THE STORY OF

Florida's Seminole Indians

By

Wilfred T. Neill

GREAT OUTDOORS PUBLISHING CO.
4747 TWENTY-EIGHTH STREET NORTH
ST. PETERSBURG, FLORIDA 33714

PUBLISHING CO.

Charlie Cypress, who died in 1963, was one of the oldest living Seminoles, carving a model of a tomahawk.

Charlie Owens, who died in 19?? was one of the oldest living Seminoles, celebrating a month of a centennial.

111

CONTENTS

CONTENTS

Acknowledgments

The portrait on Page 10 is a pencil sketch made by the author, based chiefly on the McKenney and Hall painting of Tokos Emathla. The picture on Page 58 was redrawn by the author from J. C. Tidball's 1790 sketch as reproduced in Swanton, 1946.

The illustrations on Pages 49, 51, 69, 71, and 107 were made by Bruce Mozert of Silver Springs, Florida. Mr. Mozert also made some of the photographs on Pages 75 and 87. Photo on Page 81 was made by Paul Eidem of Oslo, Norway; Photo on Page 105 by G. M. Bushman of Chicago, Illinois; Pages 67, 103 and 113 by George Lowe of Sanford, Florida; and photos on Pages 54, 61 and 77 by Charles Belden of St. Petersburg, Florida. Photographs were contributed by Deaconess Harriet M. Bedell of Glade Cross Episcopal Mission at Everglades, Florida and by Samuel Grimes, of Respess-Grimes Engraving Co., Jacksonville, Florida. The bottom row of Seminole relics on Page 20 were photographed by Ray Mills, and a print provided by Dan D. Laxson. The photograph of Indian girls was made by Robert Roess of St. Petersburg, Florida. The photograph of a cane press, was made by Carol Stryker.

The author is especially grateful to Ross Allen, who sponsored the booklet, procured many of the photographs listed above, provided valuable notes and information, and financed trips into the Seminole country. Thanks are also due to the author's wife, Joanne P. Neill, for her assistance in proofreading and preparation of both the manuscript and the finished booklet, and for assistance on various trips.

Kenneth Marmon, Seminole Indian Agent, and his staff provided much valuable information; for this they have the author's gratitude. Especial thanks are due to Deaconess Bedell, who gave the author many valuable photographs, loaned others, and supplied much useful information about the lives of the present-day Seminoles.

Much reference work was done in the Public Library of Ocala, Florida, the Library of the University of Florida, and the P. K. Yonge Library of Florida History. The respective staffs of these libraries were uniformly courteous and helpful.

Finally, thanks are due to many Seminole Indians, who in some way contributed toward the preparation of this booklet. These include Charlie Cypress, Mrs. Charlie Cypress, Albert Billie, Mrs. Albert Billie, Mary Billie, Mary Motlo, David Billie, Junior Billie, Robert Osceola, Rev. Billie Osceola, Stanley Cypress, Jim Osceola, Louise Billie, Barfield Johns, Jackie Willie, Charlie Dixie, Russell Osceola, and Lena Gopher.

BIBLIOGRAPHY

ANONYMOUS. 1941. Seminole Indians in Florida. *Fla. State Dept. of Agriculture, Tallahassee, Fla.*

ANONYMOUS. 1942. Indians in the news. *Indians at Work.* Vol. IX, Nos. 9-10: 27.

ANONYMOUS. 1948. The Seminole Indians of Florida. *U.S. Indian Service.* Pp. 1-16.

ANONYMOUS. 1951. Brief history and special problems among the Seminoles of Florida. *Seminole Indian Agency, Dania, Fla.* (mimeographed leaflet).

BARTRAM, WILLIAM. 1791. Travels through North and South Carolina, Georgia, East and West Florida. *James and Johnson,* Philadelphia, Pa.

BOYD, MARK F. 1951. The Seminole War: its background and onset. *Fla. Historical Quarterly,* Vol. XXX, No. 1: 3-113.

---------------------- 1955. Asi-Yaholo or Osceola. *Fla. Historical Quarterly,* Vol. XXXIII, Nos. 3-4: 249-305.

BULLEN, RIPLEY P. 1950. An archaeological survey of the Chattahoochee River Valley in Florida. *Jour. Washington Acad. Sciences,* Vol. XL, 103-125.

CAPRON, LOUIS. 1953. The medicine bundles of the Florida Seminole and the Green Corn Dance. *Bull.* 151, *Bureau Amer. Ethnology, Anthropological Paper* No. 35: 155-210.

CASH, W. T. 1938. The story of Florida. Vols. 1-4. *The American Historical Society, Inc., New York, N.Y.*

CATLIN, GEORGE. 1848. Illustrations of the manners, customs and condition of the North American Indians: etc. Vols. 1-2. *Henry G. Bohn, London, England.*

COE, C. H. 1898. Red patriots: the story of the Seminoles. *Editor Pub. Co., Cincinnati, Ohio.*

.... 1939. The parentage and birthplace of Osceola. *Fla. Historical Quarterly*, Vol. XVII, No. 4: 304-311.

COHEN, FELIX S. 1942. Handbook of Federal Indian Law. *U.S. Govt. Printing Office, Washington, D.C.*

CORSE, CARITA D. 1935. Shrine of the water gods: historical account of Silver Springs, Florida. *Pepper Printing Co., Gainesville, Fla.*

CUTLER, H. G. 1923. History of Florida, past and present. *Lewis Pub. Co., New York, N.Y.*

DENSMORE, FRANCES. 1932. Recording Indian music (in Explorations and field-work of the Smithsonian Institution in 1931). *Smithsonian Institution Pub.* 3134: 183-190.

.... 1933. Recording Seminole songs in Florida (in Explorations and field-work of the Smithsonian Institution in 1932). *Smithsonian Institution Pub.* 3213: 93-96.

DOVELL, J. E. 1947. The Everglades before reclamation. *Fla. Historical Quarterly*, Vol. XXVI, No. 1: 1-43.

DREW, FRANK. 1928. Florida place names of Indian origin. *Fla. Historical Quarterly*, Vol. VI, No. 4: 197-205.

FOREMAN, GRANT. 1932. Indian removal: the emigration of the five civilized tribes of Indians. *University of Okla. Press, Norman, Okla.*

.... 1934. The five civilized tribes. *University of Okla. Press, Norman, Okla.*

GIDDINGS, J. R. 1858. The exiles of Florida. *Follett, Foster and Co., Columbus, Ohio.*

GOGGIN, JOHN M. 1939. An anthropological reconnaissance of Andros Island, Bahamas. *American Antiquity*, Vol. 5, No. 1: 21-26.

.... 1940. Silver work of the Florida Seminole. *El Palacio*, Vol. 47: 25-32.

.... 1946. The Seminole Negroes of Andros Island, Bahamas. *Fla. Historical Quarterly*, Vol. XXIV, No. 3: 201-206.

.... 1951a. Beaded shoulder pouches of the Florida Seminole. *Fla. Anthropologist*, Vol. IV, Nos. 1-2: 3-17.

.... 1955. Osceola: portraits, features, and dress. *Fla. Historical Quarterly*, Vol. 33, Nos. 3-4: 161-192.

GREENLEE, ROBERT F. 1942. Ceremonial practices of the modern Seminoles. *Tequesta*, Vol. 1: 25-33.

.... 1944. Medicine and curing practices of the modern Florida Seminoles. *American Anthropologist*, Vol. 46, No. 3: 317-328.

3

.... 1952. Aspects of social organization and material culture of the Seminole of Big Cypress Swamp. *Fla. Anthropologist,* Vol. 5, Nos. 3-4: 25-31.

HODGE, FREDERICK W. 1907, 1910. (Editor) Handbook of American Indians north of Mexico. *Bureau of American Ethnology Bull.* 30, Vols. 1-2.

HRDLICKLA, ALES. 1922. The anthropology of Florida. *Fla. State Historical Society Pub.* 1, DeLand, Fla.

KROGMAN, W. M. 1935a. The physical anthropology of the Seminole Indians of Oklahoma. *Comitato Italiano per lo Studio dei Problemi della Popolazione,* 3rd ser., Vol. 2: 1-199.

.... 1935b. Vital data on the population of the Seminole Indians of Florida and Oklahoma. *Human Biology,* Vol. 7: 335-349.

.... 1948. The racial type of the Seminole Indians of Florida and Oklahoma. *Fla. Anthropologist,* Vol. 1, Nos. 3-4: 61-73.

LAXSON, D. D. 1954. An historic Seminole burial in a Hialeah midden. *Fla. Anthropologist,* Vol. 7, No. 4: 110-118.

MacCAULEY, CLAY. 1883. Personal characteristics of Florida Seminoles. *Smithsonian Misc. Collections,* Vol. 25, Washington, D.C.

.... 1887. The Seminole Indians of Florida. *5th Annual Report of the Bureau of American Ethnology,* 1883-1884: 469-531.

McKENNEY, THOMAS L. and JAMES HALL. 1933, 1934. The Indian tribes of North America. Vol. 1-3. *John Grant, Edinburgh, Scotland.*

NASH, ROY. 1930 (1931). Survey of the Seminole Indians of Florida. *Senate Document* No. 314 (71st Congress, 3rd session).

NEILL, WILFRED T. 1952. Florida's Seminole Indians. *Ross Allen's Reptile Institute, Silver Springs, Fla.*

.... 1953. Dugouts of the Mikasuki Seminole. *Fla Anthropologist,* Vol. 6, No. 3: 77-84.

.... 1954. Strange names of Florida rivers and towns. *Fla. Wildlife,* Vol. 8, No. 5: 17, 41-42, 34.

.... 1955a. The identity of Florida's "Spanish Indians." *Fla. Anthropologist,* Vol. 8, No. 2: 43-57.

.... 1955b. The site of Osceola's village in Marion County, Florida. *Fla. Historical Quarterly,* Vol. 33, Nos. 3-4: 240-246.

PORTER, KENNETH W. 1945. Notes on Seminole Negroes in the Bahamas. *Fla. Historical Quarterly,* Vol. XXIV, No. 1: 56-60.

.... 1946a. Tiger Tail. *Fla. Historical Quarterly,* Vol. XXIV, No. 3: 216-217.

4

.... 1946b. The Negro Abraham. *Fla. Historical Quarterly*, Vol. XXV, No. 1: 1-43.

.... 1947. The episode of Osceola's wife: fact or fiction? *Fla. Historical Quarterly*, Vol. XXVI, No. 1: 92-98.

.... 1949. The founder of the "Seminole Nation" — Secoffee or Cowkeeper. *Fla. Historical Quarterly*, Vol. XXVII, No. 4: 362-384.

.... 1951. The Seminole in Mexico, 1850-1861. *Hispanic American Historical Review*, Vol. 31, No. 1: 1-36.

READ, WILLIAM A. 1934. Florida place names of Indian origin and Seminole personal names. *La. State University Press, Baton Rouge, La.*

SPOEHR, ALEXANDER. 1941. Camp, clan, and kin among the Cow Creek Seminoles. *Field Museum Nat. Hist., Anthropological Ser.*, Vol. 33: 1-37.

.... 1942. Kinship system of the Seminole. *Field Museum Nat. Hist., Pub.* 513.

.... 1944. The Florida Seminole camp. *Field Museum Nat. Hist., Anthropologisal Ser.*, Vol. 33: 117-150.

SPRAGUE, J. T. 1848. The Origin, Progress and Conclusion of the Florida War. *Appleton and Co., New York, N.Y.*

STURTEVANT, WILLIAM C. 1953. Chakaika and the "Spanish Indians": Documentary sources compared with Seminole tradition. *Tequesta*, No. 13: 35-73.

.... 1954. The medicine bundles and busks of the Florida Seminole. *Fla. Anthropologist*, Vol. 7, No. 2: 31-70.

.... 1956. R. H. Pratt's Report on the Seminole in 1879. *Fla. Anthropologist*, Vol. 9, No. 1: 1-24.

SWANTON, JOHN R. 1922. Early History of the Creek Indians and their Neighbors. *Bull. 73, Bureau Amer. Ethnology.*

.... 1946. The Indians of the Southeastern United States. *Bull. 137, Bureau Amer. Ethnology.*

WARD, MARY M. 1955. The disappearance of the head of Osceola. *Fla. Historical Quarterly*, Vol. 3, Nos. 3-4: 193-201.

WILLSON, MINNIE (MOORE). 1928.. The Seminoles of Florida. *Kingsport Press, Kingsport, Tenn.*

.... 1931. Osceola, Florida's Seminole war chieftain. *Davis Pub. Co., Palm Beach, Fla.*

Foreword

Back in the 1930's, I began making trips to the Florida Everglades, to collect reptiles and other creatures for shipment to scientists and zoos, and for exhibit at the Reptile Institute. In the 'Glades I came to know the Seminole Indians; and developed a respect and admiration for these people of Florida's great swampland.

In 1935 a group of Seminoles moved to Silver Springs. Their arrival marked the return of the Seminole to his old stamping-grounds for in the vicinity of Silver Springs much Seminole history has been made.

About three miles southwest of the springs stood Fort King, the old Seminole Agency, and six miles beyond the fort was the home of Osceola, famed Seminole chief. Other chiefs, including Coe Hadjo, Taski-heniha, and Arpeika, once lived in the area.

A few miles to the northeast was Payne's Landing, where in 1832 an important treaty with the Seminoles was negotiated, and not far to the northwest lived Micanopy, head chief during the Second Seminole War.

Three miles east of Silver Springs is the Oklawaha River, which still bears the name of a Seminole band. Between the springs and the river is an old Seminole camp site where beads, gun-flints, and pottery have been found.

The Seminole families found constant, gainful employment at Silver Springs and an unprecedented opportunity to sell their handiworks. Each year many thousands of visitors have marveled at the thatched huts, the gaudy costumes, the fine handicrafts, and the simple ways of these Indians. And a great many of the visitors have wished to know more about Florida's Seminoles.

In this book the reader will find an accurate account of the Seminole Indians, their history, languages, appearance, and customs, from the time of their origin as a separate group, down to the present day.

ROSS ALLEN,
Silver Springs, Florida

CHAPTER ONE

Origin of Seminoles

A visitor to Florida is driving along a paved highway in the southern part of the state. Scarcely 30 miles away are hotels, stores, the throngs of civilization. Suddenly the driver jams on the brakes and stares in amazement. Beside the road is a wide canal, and on its still waters floats a boat, a dug-out hollowed from a single tree-trunk. In the boat stands a man, motionless as a statue. The man wears a jacket and skirt of gaudy colors arranged in an intricate design. His hair has been shaved away except for a crest across the front. In his hands is a long spear. Behind him, on the far bank of the canal, is a thatched hut without walls, nestled under a moss-hung tree.

Who is this primitive hunter? He is a Seminole Indian, an anachronism, a link with the past. He lunges suddenly with his spear and lifts from the water a large fish impaled upon its point. Along the highway the streamlined cars rush by, and overhead a jet plane roars.

Early white settlers found the southeastern United States to be inhabited by many scattered Indian tribes. A number of these tribes, mostly in Georgia, Alabama, and South Carolina, were loosely organized into what was later called the Creek Confederacy. In the early 1700's, a group of Indians, the Oconee, left their home near what is now Milledgeville, Georgia, and migrated southward. Some of them reached Florida, a few miles south of the present site of Gainesville, about 1750. The Muskogee, a leading branch of the Creek Confederacy, had a name for people such as the Oconee, who left the populous regions and lived by themselves. The name was *Sim-in-oli*, meaning "wild." This southward movement of the Oconee marked the beginning of what is now the "Seminole" group.

The original Indian inhabitants of Florida had been greatly reduced in numbers by warfare and by epidemic diseases contracted from the whites. Thus much country was left open to colonization, and the tribes of Alabama, Georgia, and South Carolina began to move southward to escape the pressure of advancing settlement. The Oconee were soon joined by other groups, including the Sawokli, Tamathli, Apalachicola, Hitchiti, and Chiaha, who had been living mostly in the Chattahoochee River area of western Georgia. All these tribes spoke a single language called Hitchiti. About 1767, the Eufaula from Alabama joined the Seminole. They spoke a different language, Muskogee. In 1788, still other Muskogee-speaking Indians from Alabama affiliated themselves with the growing Seminole group.

After the Creek War of 1813-14, the numbers of the Seminole were tripled by refugees from many tribes, mostly Muskogee-speaking people from Alabama and Georgia. To the Seminole were eventually added, also, a band of Yuchi from Georgia; Alabama tribes from the state that still bears their name; a scattering of Yamassee and Apalachee; and possibly a few of the Calusa, who originally inhabited Southwest Florida.

The Seminoles were joined, likewise, by a goodly number of run-away Negro slaves. Many of these had been originally captured from fierce African fighting tribes, such as the Ibo and Egba, Senegalese from Dakar, and the famed Ashanti or Corromantee from the Gold Coast. The Seminoles welcomed these able warriors and permitted them to form their own towns or villages. Thus, in 1821, of about 34 "Seminole" settlements 31 were occupied by Indians and 3 by Negroes.

From this alliance of many peoples rose the Seminole "tribe". During the Seminole Wars, the Muskogee-speaking Indians were dominant numerically, but the Hitchiti-speaking people continued to supply most of the leaders. A group of the latter, who came to be called the Mikasuki, were especially bitter enemies of the whites. A band of Hitchiti-speaking Indians managed to hold out in the swamps of South Florida after most of the Muskogee element had been sent to a reservation in Oklahoma. Nearly two-thirds of the present-day Seminoles in Florida are Hitchiti-speaking people, and are generally called Mikasuki to distinguish them from the Muskogee-speaking or "Cow Creek" Seminoles.

It is actually incorrect to call the Florida Seminoles a "tribe," for even today they are divided into two linguistic and four political groups. North of Lake Okeechobee, on Brighton Reservation and near Fort Drum, are the Cow Creek Seminoles. South of the lake, on the Big Cypress Reservation, are a group of Mikasukis. Along the Tamiami Trail are another group of Mikasukis, who do not wish to live on a reservation. At Dania is a third band of Mikasukis; devout Christians, they oppose pagan ways, and choose to live near the Indian Agency. Each band stages its own Green Corn Dance (except, of course, the Dania group).

Costume of a Seminole chief, about 120 years ago. Note the silver ornaments, beaded shoulder pouch, leggings, and plumed turban.

CHAPTER TWO

Attacks on the Seminole, 1812-14
and First Seminole War, 1817-18

In the early 1800's, Florida was a Spanish possession. The United States feared that the region might fall into the hands of the British, who would use it as a base for hostile operations. Also it was rather certain that, in the event of conflict, the Seminoles would not side with the Americans, whom they had no reason to like. In addition, the Seminoles held much fine country which was coveted by the whites. And finally, the plantation owners of Georgia and Alabama bitterly resented the sanctuary that the Seminoles and the Spaniards gave to escaped Negro slaves. Therefore it is not surprising to learn that, during the War of 1812, U.S. troops were sent to "punish" the Seminoles ostensibly for the crime of bringing food to the besieged city of St. Augustine. In latter 1812, an army marched into the Seminole country near the present site of Gainesville. The troops succeeded in killing King Payne, an Indian leader, but were forced to retreat after eight days.

In early 1813, an army of 400 horsemen from Tennessee joined with the American forces, under direct orders to "chastise the Indians, plunder and burn their homes and property, and drive in their cattle." Any armed Negro was to be put to death without mercy. The army was very successful in its bloody mission, and for a time the Seminole spirit was crushed. The U.S. then withdrew its troops from Florida, not wishing to antagonize Spain while that country was at war with Great Britain.

The Seminoles took little part in the Creek War of 1813-14, although they had been urged to do so by Tecumseh, the famous Shawnee Indian chief and orator, who visualized a coalition of all the southern and western tribes.

THE FIRST SEMINOLE WAR, 1817-18

Inevitably there was much ill feeling between the Seminoles and the whites. This was aggravated by a series of little "incidents" — a white man killed here; an Indian murdered there; cattle driven from the Seminole herds over the border into Georgia; the burning of a white settler's house; an Indian family captured and sold as slaves. The flames of hatred were fanned by British adventurers who encouraged and armed the Seminoles; by rival trading houses vying for Indian patronage; and by the southern plantation owners, who wished to extend their system and their holdings into Florida.

The further importation of Negro slaves into the United States had been forbidden in 1808. The value of escaped Negroes (and their descendants among the Seminoles) had risen enormously thereafter, and the Seminole country was constantly being invaded by bands of slave catchers. The invasions contributed greatly to the unrest among the Indians.

The first event of the actual war took place in latter 1817. Neamathla, chief of a Seminole village in southwestern Georgia, had warned the soldiers of a near-by fort that he would tolerate no trespassing on his hunting-grounds. In answer to such effrontery, 250 soldiers attempted to capture the villagers. The Indians resisted and then retreated, abandoning their settlement after the loss of several men and women. Inflamed by this raid, which they considered unprovoked, the Seminoles retaliated just nine days later, when they opened fire upon a boatload of 40 U.S. soldiers, 7 women, and 4 children, most of whom were killed. The Indians also looted a trading store near the mouth of the Apalachicola River and carried the clerks into captivity.

12

The American forces opposing the Seminoles were placed under the command of General Andrew Jackson. He organized about 3,000 men, more than half of which were Creek Indians led by the half-breed chieftain, Mac-Intosh. Jackson attacked the Seminoles, burning most of their towns, seizing thousands of bushels of corn, taking great numbers of horses and hogs, driving off several thousand head of cattle, and killing or capturing all who stood in his path. After subduing the Seminoles, he also attacked Spanish settlements in the state.

By the middle of 1818, the Seminoles had been quieted. The following year a treaty was negotiated whereby the ownership of Florida would be transferred from Spain to the United States. The treaty was ratified by the former country in 1820 and by the latter in 1821.

Osceola, famed war leader of the Seminoles. Redrawn by the author from George Catlin's 1838 portrait. The original was painted a few days before Osceola's death.

CHAPTER THREE

Second Seminole War, 1835-42

Unfortunately for the Seminoles, the first American governor of Florida was Andrew Jackson. He had no patience with Indians who stood in the way of white settlement. Most of the tribes of the Southeast had been exterminated or sent to "reservations" in the West; and Jackson urged that the same course be followed with the Seminoles. The latter soon heard rumors of Jackson's intentions.

Finally it was decided to herd all the Seminoles into one small tract in Central Florida. The purpose of this action was to keep the Indians away from the coast, where they might secure arms shipments. The plan was put into effect, but, needless to say, it fell far short of solving the problem. Traders, liquor vendors, slavers, agitators, adventurers—all invaded the Seminole tract. The Indians were virtually forced out of the reserved area by a tide of settlers. In 1827 the Florida Legislative Council decreed that any male Seminole found off the tract "shall receive not exceeding thirty-nine stripes on his bare back, and his gun be taken away from him". In its 1829 session, the Council stated as follows: "The present location (of the Indians) is in the pathway of our settlers and has seriously impeded the settlement of the fairest part of Florida . . ." Thus the Seminoles were forced onto the reservation and then condemned for being there.

In 1832, the Seminole leaders met the whites at Payne's Landing on the Oklawaha River, a few miles northeast of Silver Springs. Here it was agreed to send a group of Indians to what was then Arkansas (now a part of Oklahoma). They were to inspect an area set aside there for the Seminoles, and then to return and make a report to their people. Seven chiefs made the trip in 1833. Six of them were Indians and one was a Negro named Abraham. The latter served as interpreter and as a representative of the Negro towns allied with the Seminole. We may suppose that every effort was made to impress the delegates favorably. Indeed, a contemporary writer noted that the chiefs were copiously wined and dined, especially the former! In any event, while in Arkansas, they were persuaded to sign a paper promising immediate removal of all Seminoles from Florida.

Now Seminole chieftains were not autocratic; they were not empowered to sign away the lands of their people. Even so, Micanopy, head chief of the Seminoles, probably would have submitted to the removal, for he had grown old and war-weary. But a freedom-loving young warrior, named Osceola, began even then to organize a resistance element.

The Seminoles had been given until 1836 to prepare for removal, and some of the village chiefs intended to comply with orders, moving their bands to the "port of embarkation" at Tampa Bay. Not so Osceola, however. At the Fort King Indian Agency, about three miles southwest of Silver Springs, he was outspoken against the whites, and was thrown into prison for six days as a result of his words.

Shortly thereafter, six roaming Indians killed and cooked a cow. The cow, however, was claimed by a white man, who, organizing a party of friends, held the Indians at rifle point and flogged them severely. While the flogging was going on, four other Indians came upon the scene and opened fire on the white men. The fire was returned, and

16

there were several casualties on each side. With such minor incidents did the war begin.

A Seminole chief, Charley Emathla, planned to accept the conditions of removal. He sold his tribe's cattle and went to Fort King to collect his pay. Returning to his village, he was set upon and killed by Osceola, who contemptuously scattered his money in every direction. Several other chiefs immediately changed their minds about selling their cattle; while still others, fearing Osceola, hastened to the fort at Tampa Bay.

In latter 1835, the American government sent 110 soldiers to reinforce the garrison at Fort King. The men marched overland, always wary of ambush. Finally they reached a broad, open tract, and relaxed their vigilance. Here they were attacked by a band of Seminoles under a chief called Alligator, who had skilfully concealed his men behind trees and in little clumps of palmetto bushes. All the soldiers were killed except four who escaped. Only three of these eluded pursuit, and, badly wounded, made their way to safety. The Seminole head chief, Micanopy, was present at this battle. In the engagement the Seminoles were aided by a body of Negroes, seemingly headed by Abraham, who has been mentioned previously. The incident is known as the "Dade Massacre"; it took place near the present site of Bushnell, in Sumter County, Florida.

On the same day that the soldiers were wiped out, Osceola killed the general who had ordered his imprisonment at Fort King. Aided by a few Indians, he also killed another officer and five civilians, as well as looted and burned a store, all in the very sight of the fort.

Shortly thereafter, several pitched battles were fought between the Indians and the troops. The plight of the white soldiers in Florida had become desperate by the spring of 1836. Then, surprisingly, the head chief of the Seminoles, Micanopy, sent word that he was tired of war and desirous of peace. A truce was arranged, and, at the appointed time, Osceola and two other Indians approached under a white flag. The Seminoles agreed to stay south of the Withlacoochee River and to cease hostilities until arrangements satisfactory to both sides could be made. While the Indians were parleying, another body of U.S. troops approached and opened fire on them. Osceola and his two companions escaped into the brush. This episode no doubt spoiled any chance for a peaceful settlement thereafter.

By the end of 1836 there had been numerous bloody engagements, and the forces of the U.S. had won no victories of any consequence. Various armies and generals were sent against the Seminoles, but most of them accomplished little. In spite of this, however, many of the Indians were willing to be removed to reservations in the West. By the middle of 1837, even Osceola announced his readiness to emigrate, and most of the Seminole bands gathered at Tampa Bay. Here it was learned that they were to be settled among the Creek Indians—the very enemies whom they had been fighting just 20 years before. And it was rumored that their Negro allies would not be allowed to accompany them, but were to be sent into slavery. This was to be the fate, not only of escaped slaves, but of the several generations of Negroes who had been born in the villages—people who were Seminole by culture if not by race. Many of the Indians had no intention of thus abandoning their allies; and so Osceola and other young braves departed during the night, taking with them a large number of Seminoles.

About the same time that Osceola and his followers left Tampa Bay, a party of Indians attacked a lighthouse and killed the keeper. These raiders were not of the Seminole proper, but were an independent band called "Spanish Indians." Of mixed Spanish and Mikasuki descent, they had been operating fisheries on the Florida west coast, and had entered the war only when it reached their territory. The U.S. forces did not distinguish between one Indian band and another; thus hostilities were renewed.

On Christmas Day, 1837, Colonel Zachary Taylor was operating in South Florida. He commanded about 1,100 men, all regular troops except for 180 Missouri Volunteers and 70 Delaware Indians. On the northern shore of Lake Okeechobee he contacted the Seminoles, who made their stand in a saw-grass marsh. Here the mounted troops were helpless and the foot soldiers nearly so. Of Taylor's men, 27 were killed and 112 were wounded; most of these were officers. The Seminole losses were only 14.

Space does not permit a detailed account of the struggles and skirmishes thereafter. Suffice it to say that the Second Seminole War dragged through nearly eight years. The full cost of the war, including property damage, was estimated to have been over $40,000,000. Nearly 1,500 of the regular soldiers were killed, besides the losses among volunteer troops and civilians. The American forces at one time had as many as 8,866 men in the field, while the Seminoles never had more than 1,500 warriors and were never able to bring half of this into battle.

After nearly eight years of fighting, many Seminoles had been killed and others caught and sent to the West. Osceola had been captured through treachery, seized while under a flag of truce. Creek, Shawnee, Delaware, Kickapoo, Sauk, Fox, and Choctaw Indians had been recruited and sent against the Seminoles, to no avail. The Cherokee Indians, a progressive people, had tried unsuccessfully to mediate the dispute. Thirty-three outstanding Seminoles, who had come to parley with the whites and Cherokees, had been imprisoned through the same kind of trickery that ensnared Osceola. The remainder of the Seminoles, war-weary but still undefeated, drew back into the swampy reaches of the Florida Everglades

Relics of the early Seminoles. Top row: 6 fragments of trade chinaware. Second row: 3 gun flints and pistol flint; 3 trade pipe bowls of clay. Third row: 2 scrapers of bottle glass and fragment of Seminole "brushed" pottery; a typical Seminole vessel. Bottom row: mirror-compact, stone bullet mold, glass beads, gun part, silver earbob, and copper plate.

CHAPTER FOUR

Further Efforts to Remove Seminoles
1849 - 54

Even in the Everglades the Seminoles were not free from molestation. Slavers, especially, were active in the area, and many Negroes and some Indians were captured and sent into bondage. The Seminoles made a very sincere effort to maintain peace; indeed, all they asked was to be left alone. But, just as before, there were unpleasant "incidents" involving Indians and whites—a theft here, a fight there, an occasional killing. Billy Bowlegs, then chief of the Seminoles, tried desperately to prevent trouble, and even turned Indian offenders over to the whites for punishment. However, there was a continued demand from the white settlers that the Seminoles be completely removed.

About 1850 it was proposed to bribe the Seminoles into leaving Florida. Bowlegs was offered $215,000 to remove his tribe to the West. At the very mention of emigration, however, the Indians became aroused, and the subject was wisely dropped.

In 1851 the government hired a "removal specialist" who had been very successful in dispossessing the Cherokees and sending them westward. To do the same with the Seminoles, he was allowed $10,000 expenses plus $5 a day for himself, and, in addition, $800 for each warrior and $450 for each woman or child whom he sent beyond the Mississippi. His efforts, however, availed but little.

A group of Seminoles who had been previously removed to Arkansas were then brought to Florida to talk with Bowlegs and his men. But the delegation reported living conditions to be very bad in the West; and the Florida Seminoles were therefore all the more determined to remain where they were.

Next, Bowlegs and another leader were invited to make a trip to Washington, D.C., "all expenses paid". This they did, taking with them the Negro interpreter, Abraham. who was brought from the western reservation where he had been sent in 1839. They were accompanied by the "removal specialist" and his cronies. The journey was a memorable one! The oddly assorted group traveled by horses and hacks, steamboats, stagecoaches, and trains; and at hotels in Tampa, Palatka, Orange City, Savannah, and Washington the Indian chief was registered as "Mr. William B. Legs". Each member of the party had an expense account, and Abraham took advantage of his: he bought one pair of drawers, 7½ pounds of bread, 7½ pounds of sugar crackers, one pair of boots, and one plug of tobacco. The account of the "removal specialist" was considerably more extensive.

The chiefs and Abraham enjoyed the trip very much, but, upon its conclusion, they still saw no reason to move to the western reservation.

On January 12, 1853, the General Assembly of the United States passed an act decreeing as follows: "It shall be unlawful for any Indian or Indians to remain within the limits of the State (of Florida), and any Indian or Indians that may remain, or may be found within the limits of this State, shall be captured and sent west of the Mississippi."

By early 1854, the "removal specialist" had sent westward 12 Indian men and 24 women and children, at a cost to the government of $48,025 plus $5,000 for transportation. Seven of the Indians died on the trip. The "specialist" was then dismissed.

THE THIRD SEMINOLE UPRISING, 1855-58

Florida was rapidly being settled, and in the van of settlement were the engineers and the surveyors, mapping out the uncharted swamplands. In 1855 a party of surveyors penetrated far into the Big Cypress Swamp. Just two miles away was the encampment of the Seminole chief, Billy Bowlegs. Here, on an island in the swamp, the Indians had planted beans and corn, pumpkins, and a luxuriant grove of bananas. The surveyors found the garden, appropriated all the ripe fruit and vegetables, then tore down the remainder. Controlling his anger, Bowlegs approached the surveyors' camp and demanded restitution. He received neither apology nor compensation.

We may imagine the emotions that filled the breasts of the chieftain and his people. They had been hunted from place to place, declared outlaws, pushed into the heart of the wildest swamp in North America—and now, with their backs to the wall, this further indignity was thrust upon them. Grimly Bowlegs gathered his remaining warriors. The following morning, the Indians attacked the surveyors' camp, seriously wounding the officer in charge and injuring several other men. Once again, war had broken out in Florida.

During the months that followed, both Federal and State troops were thrown against the Seminoles, but to little avail. The Indians struck like a snake and retreated to the swamps before they could be engaged. They were here, there, everywhere, lurking in the dark, skulking through the brush, ready with gun, knife, or iron-tipped arrow. They cut down stragglers, hunters, soldiers, trappers; burned farmhouses; destroyed bridges, stores, crops. The unrelenting guerrilla warfare was the despair of the soldiers sent to quell it. A few Seminole villages were burned, and a few Indians met death or deportation; but in early 1858, Jefferson Davis, the Secretary of War, admitted that the Seminoles "had baffled the energetic efforts of our army to effect their subjugation and removal".

Finally, another group of Seminoles was brought from the West, and sent into the Everglades to make peace offers to Billy Bowlegs. As an inducement to emigrate, the

chief was offered $6,500 for himself, $1,000 for each of
his four sub-chiefs, $500 for each of his warriors, and $100
for every woman or child. To this proposal the weary Indian agreed. To the west went Bowlegs and 123 of his followers, plus 41 others who had been captured. One of the
Indians committed suicide en route.

Although Bowlegs had at last surrendered, the fighting spirit of the Indians was not broken. About 300 Seminoles flatly rejected the peace offer. They withdrew to
the swamps, where they waited, armed and alert, ready
to fight to the death.

In the 1880's, it looked as though a fourth Seminole
uprising was in the making. Toward the latter part of that
decade, some venturesome white men were fired upon by
a band of Seminoles in the Everglades. United States cav-
alry troops were hastily withdrawn from the West (where
they had been fighting other Indians), and were dispatch-
ed to Florida. Nothing came of the incident, and there were
no further hostilities.

The Florida Seminoles of today are the children, grand-
children, great-grandchildren and great - great - grandchil-
dren of the people who so valiantly resisted oppression a
little more than 90 years ago. Some aged Seminoles, still
alive today, can remember the time of bitter enmity between the Indians and the whites.

CHAPTER FIVE

Story of Osceola

Osceola was the most celebrated of the Seminole leaders. Little is known of his early days. He was born about 1803, most likely around the Tallapoosa River, in northern Alabama, in the territory of the Muskogee or Creek Indians. He was not a full-blood, for his maternal great-grandfather had been a Scotchman, James McQueen. This McQueen was a trader who had married a Creek Indian woman; and one of McQueen's half-breed children, Ann, eventually married a man named Copinger. It is inferred that Copinger was white or half-breed and probably of Spanish origin. Ann McQueen Copinger's daughter, Polly, was the mother of Osceola. When Osceola was a lad, his mother was married to a white trader named William Powell; and Osceola was often thought to be Powell's child. However, there is some reason to believe that Powell was Polly Copinger's second husband, and that her first husband, a Creek Indian, was the real father of Osceola. At any rate, Osceola was a Creek Indian by culture and by inclination; he spoke little English and publicly disavowed any white ancestry.

It was said that Osceola, while no more than 10 or 11 years old, participated in or at least went through the

Creek War of 1813-14. In 1818, he and his mother were captured by Andrew Jackson's soldiers, but were subsequently released. Eventually the two went to Fort King, about 3 miles southwest of Silver Springs, and settled a few miles from the fort. Here young Osceola grew up to be a Seminole, although he was a Creek by birth.

As a young man, Osceola excelled at running, hunting, and wrestling. The Seminoles, like other southeastern Indians, were fond of a rough and vigorous sort of ball game similar to lacrosse; and Osceola became a noted ball player. But beyond winning renown as an athlete, he did nothing to attract special notice in his youth.

One of the most familiar anecdotes about Osceola is the least authenticated. During the early 1800's, bands of slavers often rambled into Florida, capturing Negroes to be sold in Georgia. These slavers at times seized upon Indians as well. It has often been said that such a fate befell Osceola's wife; and that this incident brought about Osceola's later enmity toward the whites. The episode is related in many history books, but has no basis in fact. Apparently it first appeared in print in an anti-slavery magazine. Here it was stated that Osceola's wife was the daughter of a runaway slave, and that the whole Seminole War really resulted from the institution of slavery. This fine piece of propaganda was spread widely in anti-slavery periodicals, some of which stated that it was Osceola's mother who was carried off. Later, a Negro author elaborated the story still further, stating that both Osceola and his wife were children of runaway slaves! Such, however, was not the case, and the whole "episode of Osceola's wife" seems to have been a mere fabrication intended to arouse anti-slavery sentiment.

As a matter of fact Osceola had two wives, in accordance with Seminole custom at that time. He also had several children. Little is known of Osceola's family; it is uncertain whether they remained in Florida or were sent to Oklahoma.

Osceola first began to attract attention about 1832, when he opposed the plan to send all Seminoles westward. According to tradition, he was present on one occasion when a group of Indians were told that they must sign a treaty submitting to the removal. Eyes flashing, Osceola drew his knife, stabbed it through the treaty paper which was lying on the council table, and exclaimed, "This is the only treaty I will ever make with the whites!" (A statue of Osceola, looking out over Silver Springs, perpetuates this dramatic gesture). Apparently the tale has some basis in fact; the treaty paper with Osceola's "signature", a knife gash, is preserved today.

In 1835, at the Fort King Agency, Osceola was outspoken for Indian rights, and bitterly contemptuous of the white man's treaties and promises. The Indian Agent, General Wiley Thompson, promptly had Osceola thrown in jail. Here he was bound so tightly that his wrists bore scars two years later. After six days he was released.

Osceola must have sworn revenge against the general who had him imprisoned. It would seem that he haunted the woods around the fort, off and on, for months thereafter, watching for the chance that he was sure would come.

In early 1836 he killed a Seminole chief who had sold cattle to the whites at the fort. About this time he also attended a conference with the soldiers. While Osceola and two other Indians were parleying under a flag of truce, they were fired upon by a body of troops and were forced to flee into the bushes.

Late in 1836 Osceola found the opportunity he had been awaiting for so long. One afternoon, the Indian Agent, accompanied by a lieutenant, strolled out for a little walk. From behind trees stepped Osceola and several other Indians. They killed the two officers, and then attacked a store beside the fort. Under the very noses of the soldiers they killed the occupants of the store, looted the building, and set it afire.

From then on, Osceola's rise to power was rapid. It is interesting to note that he was not a chief, either by descent or by election. He became a leader solely through his personal ability. His influence grew so great that he was soon able to flout the desires of the Seminole head chief, Micanopy, who was opposed to warfare with the whites.

In the summer of 1837, Osceola announced his readiness to emigrate, and brought his followers to Tampa Bay.

Here, displeased with the terms of removal, he persuaded many of the Seminoles to return to their villages and continue the struggle.

Osceola led and inspired the Seminoles until latter 1837. At that time he agreed to another parley, entering an army camp near St. Augustine, Florida, under a flag of truce. Here he was knocked on the head, bound, and imprisoned. Shortly thereafter, he was sent to a dungeon at Fort Moultrie, South Carolina. He lived but a few months in prison, dying in January, 1838. The direct cause of his death was a severe inflammation of the throat and tonsils.

The indignities heaped upon Osceola did not end with his death. In the last days of his illness the Indian had been attended by an army physician, a certain Dr. Frederick Weedon. Weedon's wife was the sister of Wiley Thompson, the Indian Agent whom Osceola had killed. As soon as Osceola died, Weedon cut off his head. He let the head remain in the casket, the cut hidden by a scarf; and later he found opportunity to smuggle the head away. The doctor's great-granddaughter recently published an account of the episode. She wrote, "Dr. Weedon was an unusual man . . . he used to hang the head of Osceola on the bedstead where his three little boys slept, and leave it there all night as punishment for misbehavior." He must have been unusual indeed. He eventually gave the head to a son-in-law, who in turn presented it to a surgeon. The surgeon's collection of specimens was subsequently lost by fire. Dr. Weedon also obtained some of Osceola's clothing, ornaments, and other possessions; a few of these are still in existence, having been handed down to Weedon's descendants.

Osceola's headless body was buried at Fort Moultrie, under a stone on which were inscribed the words "Patriot and Warrior". In 1950 there was a demand that the chief's remains be brought back to Florida, the state with which he is historically associated. Surviving descendants of Osceola have laid claim to the body. The Seminole elders, leery of dealing with white people, have opposed the move, At the present writing, the issue is still unsettled.

MEANING OF THE NAME "OSCEOLA"

A Seminole child received a name that had been previously used in the family, or was given a name made up on the spot, or was simply called "Little Boy" or "Little Girl".

But as a boy grew up and became a warrior, he received another name, a "ceremonial name" bestowed on him as a result of some personal peculiarity or some incident in his life. Many of the Indian leaders became known to history by their ceremonial names, not their actual names. This was the case with Osceola.

Before a war party set out, its members gathered for a ceremony. An important part of the ceremony was the drinking of a liquid brewed from the leaves of various plants. The decoction was dark in color, rather like strong tea in flavor, and rich in caffeine. It acted as an emetic, laxative, and diuretic. The white man called the liquid "the black drink"; the Seminole name was *"asi"*.

As the warriors drank of the *asi*, they emitted quavering calls. These calls were termed *"yaholo"*, after the name of the spirit thought to preside over such ceremonies. The young Indian who was destined to lead the Seminoles was called Asi-yaholo, which may be interpreted as "Black-drink Crier". The name was corrupted by the whites to "Osceola". A rather similar combination of sounds meant "rising sun", and Osceola was also known as "The Rising Sun", but this interpretation was incorrect.

It may be mentioned in passing that the "black drink" ceremony was not confined to the Seminoles, but was practiced in some form by most of the southeastern tribes. The brew is still made and drunk by the Florida Seminoles at their annual Green Corn Dance.

(Upper left) Mrs. Squirrel Jumper and family at Glade Cross Mission.
(Upper right) Deaconess Harriet Bedell and two of her Seminole friends.
(Lower left) Johnnie Osceola and family. (Lower right) Seminole corn
grinder and sifter.

CHAPTER SIX

Other Seminole Leaders

One hears a great deal about Osceola, but little of the other Seminole leaders. A brief account of Seminole chiefs may be of interest. One of the earliest Seminole leaders, in the 1700's, was Seecoffee. He was the son of that remarkable Indian, Emperor Brims of the Creek Nation. Seecoffee is generally thought to have been the same chief whom the whites later called The Cowkeeper, on account of his large cattle herds. Cowkeeper's town, known as Cuscowilla, was located near the present hamlet of Micanopy, about 10 miles south of Gainesville, Florida. Cowkeeper was succeeded by King Payne, whose name is perpetuated in Payne's Prairie and Payne's Landing. King Payne was probably the son of Cowkeeper's sister, in accordance with the Seminole method of reckoning descent. Toward the latter 1700's, King Payne was a prominent figure and was much respected by the whites. He was killed in 1812 by a group of United States soldiers. Payne seems to have been succeeded for a time by his brother, Bolek, whom the whites called Bowlegs (not the later Billy Bowlegs). Another Seminole who came into prominence after Payne's death

was Solachoppo, called Long Tom by the white men. Solachoppo was probably a brother-in-law of Payne and Bowlegs. He died early, and was succeeded by his younger
brother, Sint-chakkee, known as the Pond Governor by
the whites. Sint-chakkee became famous in history as Micanopy, which was a title ("top chief") rather than a name.
Micanopy was a very influential leader, but he seems to
have left matters mostly in the hands of his Negro "slave",
Abraham, and an Indian called Jumper or Otee Amathla.
Micanopy's brother-in-law, called Amathla or King Philip,
was a prominent leader of the Seminoles on the St. John's
River in the early 1800's. King Philip's son, known as Coacoochee or The Wildcat, would not have been reckoned a
chief. However, he rose to power as a leader of the more
belligerent Seminole faction, especially after the capture
of Osceola. The latter, most famous Seminole leader, has
been discussed previously. An outstanding Mikasuki chief
was Tokos Emathla (shown in the portrait on Page 10),
called John Hicks or Hext by the whites. The son of Tokos
Emathla was known as Uchee Billy; he led a band of
Uchee (Yuchi) Indians who had associated themselves
with the Seminoles. Other Mikasuki leaders were Capixty
Mico (also called Cappichimico, Kenhagee, or King Hadjo), the war-chief Cochi Tustenuggee, and Tuski-heniha.
Neamathla (also known as Nehe Marthla or Innemathla)
captained a Mikasuki group although he was a Creek Indian by birth. A contemporary of Neamathla was Yamassee
Mico, leader of a band of Yamassee Indians who were al-
lied with the Seminoles. Other outstanding contemporaries
of Neamathla, in the early 1800's, were Lafarka or John
Blount (for whom Blountstown, Florida, is named), The
Mulatto King or Vaca Pechassie, Emathlochee, Econchati
Mico, and Chefixico of the Tallahassee band. The so-called
Spanish Indians were led by Chekika, a man of gigantic
stature.

Among the Seminole chiefs favoring emigration in the
1830's were Chalo Amathla, his brother Holata Amathla,
Foke-lustee Hadjo or Black Dirt, and Otulke Ohala or Big
Warrior. Toward the end of the Second Seminole War, a
Mikasuki named Arpeika or Sam Jones came into power.
He lived to a great age, and the ruins of his settlement,
deep in Big Cypress Swamp, are still shown on most Flor-

ida maps as "Sam Jones' Old Town". A contemporary of Sam Jones, and the last Seminole to lead his people in battle, was Holata Mico or Billy Bowlegs who finally surrendered in 1858. At about the time that Billy Bowlegs was sent to the Oklahoma reservation, thence also went a subchief, Thlocklo Tustenuggee or Fish Warrior, better known as Tigertail. This leader deserted the reservation, fleeing to Mexico; and after the Seminole Wars ended he apparently returned to Florida, where he settled on the outskirts of Miami and lived to an extreme old age.

There have been no recognized Seminole chiefs for many years. Micanopy, head chief during the Seminole Wars, was probably the last man to exert influence over both the Muskogee and Hitchiti elements of the Seminole. Such men as Osceola and Coacoochee the Wildcat were leaders but not chiefs in the usual sense. Many present-day Seminoles consider Billy Bowlegs to have been the last chief.

The Seminole chiefs of early days were not autocratic. In conjunction with the tribal councils they could punish infractions of Seminole law, but beyond this they could not go. They could lead, recommend, and advise, but could not coerce or demand. This was brought out many times during the Seminole Wars. For example, seven leaders agreed to the removal of the whole tribe to the West, but the bulk of the people immediately repudiated the agreement. When Micanopy, the head chief, opposed warfare with the whites, such men as Osceola openly defied him and rallied their own supporters. The Seminole way was a democratic one, emphasizing individual freedom of action.

In recent years the Seminoles have been governed by three tribal councils, one for the Cow Creek Indians, another for the Dania group, and a third for the remainder of the population. Each council member has an equal voice in all decisions made, although each council has one man who is recognized as the leader. No single Indian could really be called a Seminole chief today, even though the newspapers often confer the title on some of the Osceolas or other prominent Seminoles.

The Seminoles are understandably secretive about the tribal councils. Each council meets annually a day or two before the Green Corn Dance. No outsider is permitted to attend, and no white man knows how much power the council wields. The general opinion is that, in the last few years, severe punishments have not been meted out. However, as late as 1938, a Seminole council carried out a death sentence.

CHAPTER SEVEN

The Spanish Indians

Our section on Seminole history might close with a few additional remarks about the Spanish Indians.

Just who were these people? Not a last remnant of the Calusa, as many students have suspected. They were an independent band of Hitchiti-speaking Seminole who, back in the 1700's, moved out of southwestern Georgia and started down the west coast of Florida. Some time before 1769 they reached Charlotte Harbor, near present-day Punta Gorda, and established friendly relations with Spanish fishermen there. It is possible that they met a few Calusa Indians, also; but by and large they were mixed-blood Seminole and Spanish.

As time went by, these Indians departed more and more from the traditional Seminole ways. Under the direction of the Spaniards they manned small fishing-boats, sailing out into the Gulf to drop their nets. Each year they took their catch down to Havana, Cuba, in order to sell it. Here they also bartered for Spanish produce. Many of them were baptized in Havana, and adopted Spanish names. No

35

doubt they learned to speak Spanish, but they did not forget their own Hitchiti language.

Part of the year, when the fish were not running, these Indians dwelt in little communities along the Florida coast. They did not build substantial cabins as did the other Seminoles at that time; palm-thatched huts sufficed in the warm subtropical climate of the lower west coast. They raised corn, peas, and pumpkins in typical Seminole fashion; but from the West Indies they obtained bananas, limes, coconuts, and pineapples. They also hunted, fished, and gathered coontie roots to make into starch.

The Spanish Indians continued to occupy their fishing settlements while European nations squabbled over Florida. They were not completely isolated, however. From time to time they had dealings with their kinsmen who dwelt farther inland, and often took wives from the Seminole proper. After the United States gained control of Florida, several influential Americans went to the west coast to operate fishing fleets, employing the Spanish Indians for this purpose.

The Spanish Indians were not affected by the early attacks on the Seminole, nor did they take part in the First Seminole War. They entered the Second Seminole War only when it reached their area, in 1837. Their leader or war chief at this time was a man called Chakaika (often spelled Chekika). This Indian led a hundred or so warriors. His first hostile act was to attack a lighthouse and kill the keeper. Thereafter, Chakaika's band cast their lot with the other warring Seminoles. In 1838 they joined forces with another Seminole band and fell upon a body of soldiers who were camped on the Caloosahatchee River. In 1840 they attacked the Perrine settlement on Indian Key, a tiny island 20 miles south of the Florida mainland. Later in that year they were surprised by soldiers under Colonel W. S. Harney. Chakaika was killed, his family captured, his band dispersed.

The Spanish Indians who remained in Florida, withdrew into the Everglades and Big Cypress Swamp, affiliating themselves with the other Seminoles there. In time their separate identity was lost, but their history was not forgotten by the Seminoles.

CHAPTER EIGHT

Life of the Early Seminoles

The life of the early Seminoles must have been quite different from that of the present-day ones. When they first came to Florida, the Seminoles were an agricultural and pastoral people. They built their large villages on the higher ground, often selecting hilltops covered with live-oaks. Of course, they chose a site with drinking water in the vicinity, and with nearby grassy meadows where horses and cattle could be pastured. A village might own several thousand head of stock, as well as numerous hogs and chickens. Fields were cleared and crops planted. Corn was the most important crop; it could be roasted, made into grits, or ground into meal. Peas, beans, pumpkins, sweet potatoes, and watermelon were also grown. In Central Florida oranges were planted about the villages, while farther north peaches were grown.

An early traveler in Florida has left us a description of the Seminole town called Cuscowilla, which stood not far from present-day Gainesville. There were about 30 families in the town, and each family owned at least two small houses. One house was partitioned into a sleeping room and a cook room; the other, a two-story affair, included a potato storehouse, a granary, and a room where visitors were entertained. This last, the reception room, was on the second floor; it was pleasant and airy during the hot summer, and the family head sometimes elected to sleep there. Between the two houses was a square yard encompassed by a low bank of earth. This yard was carefully swept. In some Seminole towns a family might construct three or even four buildings, and these were always arranged around the sides of a square. In the center of the village there was a public square, with ceremonial structures inclosing two, three, or four sides. The buildings were of logs and poles, and were roofed with shingles of long-lasting cypress bark.

The possessions of the early Seminoles were by no means limited to items they could personally manufacture. In fact, the Indians were rapidly giving up many old crafts, relying on material obtained from the Spanish, the British, and the Americans. There were quite a few traders operating in the Seminole country, and the Indians made long trips for the purpose of barter.

SEMINOLE ARCHEOLOGY

Historical accounts tell us about the broader outlines of eary Seminole life, but seldom provide many details. The present-day Seminoles can supply some additional data from their traditional knowledge. However, many questions about Seminole life cannot be answered from either historical or traditional sources; and for further information one must turn to another scientific discipline, archeology.

Archeology is often thought of as being concerned with prehistoric man, but the application of archeological methods to historic Indian village sites has produced valuable results. Seminole archeology is a new development; as recently as 1948 the Seminole Period in Florida was known from historical sources alone. Then a number of early Seminole or Lower Creek sites were discovered in the valley of the Chattahoochee River near the Florida-Georgia boundary. Among them was the town of Econchatti Mico, a Creek chief who later became Seminole.

Next, an old trading post on the St. Johns River was located and excavated; it yielded numerous items that had been intended for the Seminole trade. A Seminole burial, with a large quantity of grave goods, was found near Gainesville. Material of the Seminole period was recovered from the site of Fort Gadsden; from Middleburg in Clay County, Florida; from near Winter Park; from Fort King, three miles east of Ocala; and from a Seminole village site near Silver Springs. Osceola's town, known to have been just a few miles from Ocala, was located precisely through early deeds and land grants. The site of the famous Indian's village had been plowed up annually for many years, and items dating from the time of Seminole occupation were scattered over the ground. Just in the last year or two, various other Seminole towns and camp sites (including a few Spanish Indian settlements) have been located and many interesting objects recovered.

Thus it is now possible to describe certain material possessions of the early Seminoles. Obviously they were well supplied with trade goods. Chinaware, glass bottles, clay pipes, flint-lock guns and pistols, musket balls and smaller lead shot, trade beads of glass, mirrors, nails, and screws, sabers, hoes, knives, bullet molds, pipe tomahawks of iron, kettles, cloth, paint, files, rasps, silver and copper ornaments, coins, needles, and many other objects have been recovered from Seminole sites in North and Central Florida. Chinaware traded to the Seminoles included various English, American Colonial and Early American varieties, such as creamware, Delft wares, flower-painted and transfer-printed Staffordshire china, plain white ironware, blue or green featheredge, and Oriental porcelain. Today such wares often are prized antiques, but in early days they were cheap trade items. The Seminoles had so much trade goods that it is sometimes difficult to tell the site of a Seminole village from that of an early white settlement. Usually, a Seminole site will yield faceted beads of glass, and various ornaments typical only of these Indians. (The silver earbob, shown on page 20, is typically Seminole in Florida.) Even more definitive is the presence of pottery which the Seminoles made themselves. As late as the 1820's, and probably for two or three decades thereafter, the Seminoles were making some pottery in the aboriginal fashion. This ware was easily distinguished from those of the white man and also from those of the earlier tribes in Florida. Some pots of Seminole manufacture were highly polished, and variegated with black and cream as a result of the firing technique; others were brushed while still soft with a bundle of stiff fibers, leaving the surface with numerous fine scorings.

In many ways the culture of the early Seminoles resembled that of other Southeastern Indians. The whites once grouped the Seminole, the Creek, the Choctaw, the Chickasaw, and the Cherokee as "The Five Civilized Tribes". Of course, each of these tribes had certain characteristic beliefs and ways of doing things, but there were broad similarities among them as regards clothing styles, dwellings, village layout, weapons and tools, household utensils, crop plants and agricultural practices, economy, folklore, ceremonies, social organization, and so on. In other words, the life of the early Seminoles was fairly typical of Southeastern Indians generally. Then, after the wars with the white man, the Seminoles dropped briefly from view. When they emerged again, it was with a remarkably different culture — one somewhat reminescent of West Indian or even South American tribes. Cabins were abandoned and thatched huts adopted; large villages were replaced by family camps; the hammock became almost a standard item of household furniture; hunting, fishing, and gathering became more important, agriculture much less so; graters were often made, and used in the preparation of various root crops; rubber was made from the milky latex of the strangler-fig; pineapples, guavas, coconuts, bananas, even taro and cassava were grown about the camps; dugout canoes were often fitted with mast and sail. It may be that certain new ideas, new ways of doing things, were brought to the Seminole proper by the Spanish Indians, who had been in contact with the West Indies, with widely-traveled Spaniards, and perhaps with a last remnant of the aboriginal Calusa.

Further archeological study and more intensive search for early documents are certain to throw additional light on the transitional period, and to explain the origin of various present-day Seminole customs.

CHAPTER NINE

The Life of the Present-Day Seminoles
The Everglades, Home of the Seminoles

With the exception of the Silver Springs group, the Seminole Indians of Florida live in the lower portion of the state, mainly in the great marshy tracts called the Everglades and Big Cypress Swamp. Some idea of this region must be gained before we can understand the Seminole's present manner of life.

More than halfway down the Florida peninsula is Lake Okeechobee, second largest body of fresh water lying wholly within the United States. Southward from Lake Okeechobee, the Everglades extend in a broad sweep, 100 miles long and 50 to 70 miles wide, to the southwestern tip of the state. This is a vast expanse of saw-grass, a wilderness of saw-toothed leaf blades, higher than a man's head, clustered thick as a wheat field, rooted in muck and nearly stagnant water. Monotonously the saw-grass stretches for mile on mile, broken only by scattered clumps of palms and wax-myrtle bushes. A few canals and numerous alligator trils form a network of shallow channels through the inhospitable vegetation. Toward the southern half of the

'Glades are many islands, thickly wooded with trees and vines growing in tropical profusion.

Along the southwestern coast of Florida the Everglades dip gently toward the sea. Here innumerable channels cut the land into the Ten Thousand Islands. No wilder region exists in the United States. West of the Everglades lies Big Cypress Swamp, with uncounted thousands of shallow ponds overgrown with dwarf cypress. Scattered among the ponds are slightly higher areas covered with pines and coarse wire-grass. Northwest of Lake Okeechobee is Indian Prairie, a patchwork of pine and wire-grass, treeless palmetto flats, and swampy ponds, set in a matrix of palm savanna. East of the Everglades, toward the coast, the land rises somewhat and here one finds dry pine woods and stretches of thick, scrubby vegetation.

As might be expected, the great wooded tracts of South Florida harbor many species of animal life. In this area is to be found the Florida panther, closely related to the western mountain lion. The black bear is common, as are the wildcat, deer, gray fox, and otter. Smaller animals include the opossum, raccoon, mink, spotted skunk, gray squirrel, fox squirrel, round-tailed water rat, marsh rabbit, and cottontail rabbit. In the Ten Thousand Islands region is found the manatee or sea-cow.

Bird life is abundant. Egrets, herons, coots, gallinules, rails, wood ibis, and white ibis are commonly seen about ponds and marshes. Overhead soar hawks, kites, caracaras, and magnificent bald eagles, while in the brush are flocks of wild turkeys and coveys of quail. Smaller birds—doves, kingfishers, woodpeckers, warblers, grackles, red-winged blackbirds, and many others—are numerous.

In the swamps and lakes dwell bullfrogs, alligators, harmless water snakes and poisonous cottonmouth moccasins, terrapins, snapping turtles, and soft-shelled turtles. About the wooded islands and grassy savannas live blacksnakes, orange rat snakes, king snakes, 8-foot indigo snakes, and deadly coral snakes. In the higher areas the diamondback rattlesnake is sometimes encountered. About the brackish inlets and estuaries of the lower west coast, the Florida crocodile occurs.

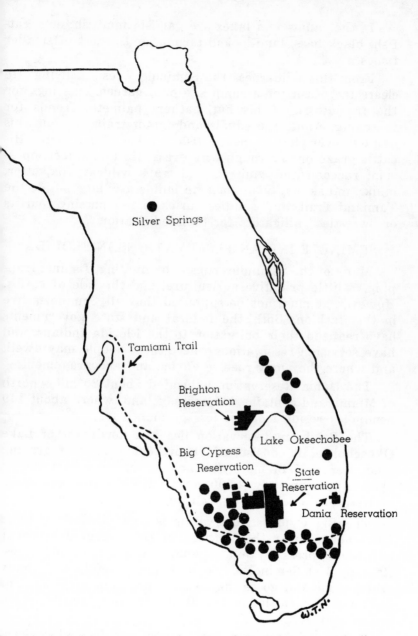

Solid circles indicate approximate locations of Seminole camps and villages in Florida. Silver Springs and the various reservations are labeled. Not all villages are inhabited simultaneously.

Silver Springs

Tamiami Trail

Brighton Reservation

Big Cypress Reservation

Lake Okeechobee

State Reservation

Dania Reservation

W.T.N.

In the canals and lakes are garfish, mudfish, eels, catfish, black bass, land-locked tarpon, and a host of smaller fishes.

From this wilderness the Seminole wrests a living. He clears the brush for a camp site or a garden, cuts logs for the framework of his hut, gathers palmetto fronds for thatching. Along the canals and 'gator trails he poles his dug-out, ever alert to spear a fish or seize upon a turtle. His cattle graze on the rough-wire grass. He hunts deer, opossum, raccoon and squirrel, and traps wildcat, fox, otter, mink, and skunk. Sometimes he builds a village beside the Tamiami Trail, and peddles curios to the passing tourists or "wrestles" alligators for their edification.

SEMINOLE INDIAN RESERVATIONS IN FLORIDA

Many of the Seminoles subsist by hunting, fishing, trapping, a little primitive agriculture, and the sale of curios. However, it must not be supposed that all Seminoles live in this fashion. Both the federal and state governments have realized their obligation to the Florida Indians, and have set aside reservations where these people may dwell, and where they may receive advice and encouragement.

The Dania Reservation is located about 20 miles north of Miami, and contains 445 acres of land, where about 149 Seminoles reside more or less permanently.

The Brighton Reservation lies just northwest of Lake Okeechobee. It consists of about 36,925 acres of grazing land. Here 175 or more Seminoles live, for a part of the year. Approximately 4,300 head of Indian-owned cattle, of Hereford stock, are grazed on this reservation.

The Big Cypress Reservation is located south of Lake Okeechobee, near the junction of the Everglades proper and Big Cypress Swamp. It comprises about 42,663 acres. Roughly 100 Seminoles live here permanently and many others come and go as they wish. More than 1,400 head of Indian-owned cattle, mixed Brahman and "scrub" stock are grazed here.

Dania, Brighton and Big Cypress are federal reservations.

The state of Florida has also set aside lands for the Seminole. The first state reservation consisted of 99,200

44

acres in that forbidding wilderness, the Ten Thousand Islands region. In 1930, a U.S. Commissioner, investigating the living conditions of the Seminoles, visited this reservation. He described it as follows: "Its average elevation above sea level is 13 inches, and . . . there are 13 mosquitoes to the cubic inch of atmosphere. In the wet season it is very wet, and . . . the dry season is also very wet."

Just a few years ago, the southwestern portion of Florida was set aside as the Everglades National Park. The park boundaries completely encompassed the state "reservation", and so, once again, the Seminoles were forced to move.

They were then given another tract of land, in the heart of the Everglades, adjacent to the Big Cypress settlement. This reservation contains 104,800 acres of swamp and marsh. Portions of the area are now used by the Seminoles, at times, for hunting and for the grazing of cattle; but few of the Indians dwell there permanently, since most of the state reservation is under water for the greater portion of the year. In 1951, it was learned that more than half of this tract would be taken away from the Seminoles, in connection with some proposed drainage projects that might render the land unfit for use.

At first glance it would seem that the Seminoles have had a considerable acreage set aside for them. However, only a small fraction of this acreage is usable land. The state reservation is really a vast, shallow lake with scattered bogs and mucky little islands. Much of the Big Cypress Reservation is flooded during the rainy season (May through October), and parts are swampy or completely inundated at other times as well. The Dania Reservation is small, and provides little but room for housing and pasturage for a few horses. Only the Brighton Reservation includes a considerable acreage of fairly dry land, although portions are often submerged during the summer.

The reservations are not forested. The Brighton Reservation has no timber of commercial value. On Big Cypress there are little stands of pine, so scattered that they would yield less than 1,000 board feet per acre. Most of the cypress trees on this reservation are not the stately bald cypress, but the dwarf or pond cypress, the trunks of which are usually no more than 9 or 10 inches in diameter. Timber authorities estimate that the reservation would yield only 23 to 24 board feet of cypress per acre.

The various reservations, both federal and state, are under the jurisdiction of the Seminole Indian Agency at Dania, Florida. The Dania Agency is under the jurisdiction of the Muskogee (Oklahoma) Agency, which also handles Creek and Seminole affairs in the west.

Indians on these reservations are not supported by the government; they must work for everything they receive. But they do get valuable advice and assistance. They are encouraged to become economically independent through cattle-raising and truck farming. They are taught trades and crafts, and receive medical attention. Schools are provided for both children and adults.

CHAPTER TEN

Seminoles Off the Reservations

More than half of the Florida Seminoles do not choose to live on the reservations. They build their villages in the relatively unsettled tract just northeast of Lake Okeechobee, in the Big Cypress Swamp west of the reservations, and along or near the Tamiami Trail. A few dwell in commercial camps near Miami. Several families live at Silver Springs.

The accompanying map (Page 43) shows the approximate locations of Seminole camps, villages, and reservations in Florida. It must not be assumed that all these areas are occupied simultaneously or constantly. Many families move about quite a bit, and often prefer to erect a new village than to reoccupy one that has been abandoned for any length of time.

Nearly all of the Florida Seminoles, except the Silver Springs group, reside in the counties of St. Lucie, Okeechobee, Glades, Hendry, Collier, Dade, and Broward. In recent times there have also been a few settlements farther north, in Indian River and Brevard counties; and sometimes the Seminoles hunt northward into Highlands and

47

Osceola counties. There have been one or two settlements in Martin County, and a few families for a time occupied a commercial camp in Pinellas County.

The swamps of South Florida are vanishing. Drainage projects, some of them ill-advised, have removed the lush vegetation and the wildlife from great tracts. Each year uncounted thousands of acres go up in smoke; for the rich, peaty soil of the Everglades, once drained, will burn down to bedrock if ever set alight. Roads, farms, and cattle ranches are constantly encroaching on the domain of the Seminoles, who tend to abandon their outlying settlements and fall back toward Big Cypress, the Okeechobee region, and the heart of the 'Glades.

In recent years, various Seminoles from the Oklahoma reservation have visited their brethren in the Everglades, and, more important, several Florida Seminoles have made trips to Oklahoma.

As mentioned previously, Seminoles are not supported by the government; they must work for all they receive. In 1936 the government furnished the tribe with a herd of beef cattle, repayable in kind. The "tribes" have been meeting their repayments to the government each year. Both the Brighton and the Big Cypress groups have now completed their payments. From the tribal enterprise herds an Indian may borrow cattle. The individual is charged 3% interest, based on the appraised value of the cattle at the time of borrowing. Livestock promises to become an important industry with the Seminoles and may some day allow many of them to become economically independent. At the present writing (March, 1956), there are about 4,300 head of cattle on the Brighton Reservation and 1,400 on Big Cypress.

Needless to say, cattle raising in the hot and humid marshes of South Florida presents many problems. The federal government has provided an extension worker who supervises and instructs the Indians in general herd management. Under his direction, the Seminoles carry on pasture rotation, controlled breeding, the construction of mineral boxes, the weaning of yearlings, screw-worm control, and other up-to-date practices. Trustees are elected by the

Charlie Cypress carves a model of a Seminole dugout, while his family sews colorful garments.

Indians to share in the management of the herds. Handling of the herds is done by Seminole range riders.

On the Brighton Reservation there are 10 tribally-owned horses; and 15 or 20 families have their own saddle horses and milk cows. Many of the Big Cypress and Dania Seminoles own saddle horses, also.

On the Big Cypress Reservation there are 14 families owning hogs. Most of these hogs are the common "range" type, and are destined for home consumption by the Indians. However, a few hogs are sold on the market every year. Each family receives an income of about $300 from these sales. On the Brighton Reservation there are 39 families owning hogs, mostly "range" hogs but a few of the Hampshire breed. Each family receives about $400 annually from the sale of these animals. Many Seminole families keep chickens, also.

The Seminoles practice comparatively little agriculture. This is due in part to the difficulty of raising crops in the flooded and insect-infested swamps, and in part to the Indian's preference for hunting, fishing, and the gathering of wild foods. The Mikasukis, especially, scorn agriculture. However, many families have little garden plots, where they raise beans, corn, pumpkins, tomatoes, bananas, guavas, sugar cane, and other crops for home consumption. The total land area farmed by the Seminoles in Florida is probably less than 200 acres.

Some of the Seminoles find their own jobs in the labor market. Both men and women work at the harvesting of truck farm products, such as tomatoes, potatoes, beans and other vegetables. A number find employment in the extensive gladiolus industry of South Florida. Others work for county and state road departments, or in sawmills, construction companies, and lumber yards. Several have been employed as mechanics in a tractor shop, and some of the youths work in gasoline stations. About 15 Seminoles find employment as range riders for the tribal enterprise herds, and a dozen others work on the reservation road project as laborers, truck drivers, bulldozer operators, and mechanics. Some employers have remarked that they would hire more Seminoles than they do, if the Indians only

Hewing logs to form the framework of a new hut.

understood more about labor unions and the complexities of the white man's civil law.

Relatively few of the Seminoles have year-'round jobs; generally there is an "off-season" during which time they subsist by hunting, fishing, the gathering of wild fruits and vegetables, and the manufacture of curios for sale to tourists. The Seminoles market most of the frog-legs sold in the Miami area, and derive a good revenue from this source. A number of Indians own air-boats—large, flat-bottomed craft powered by air propellors—with which they glide over the shallow waters in search of elusive bullfrogs. Bee-keeping, trapping, cane grinding, and other minor industries exist among the Seminoles.

A good many families make their living, or a part of it, through commercial camps. These camps may be established by the Seminoles themselves, usually on the Tamiami Trail, or may be operated at or in conjunction with some amusement park or other tourist center.

Many of the Seminole families have craft work for sale, including costume dolls, skirts, aprons, men's shirts, beadwork, wood carvings, basketry, etc. These articles often are of fine workmanship, and quite rightly command good prices. The intricately patterned garments, made from hundreds of bits of cloth, are real collectors' items. For several years an Arts and Crafts organization has been functioning on the Brighton Reservation, for the purpose of buying and selling articles of Seminole handiwork.

CHAPTER ELEVEN

Arts and Crafts

One sometimes hears the statement that Seminole arts and crafts are few. This is not actually the case. Although they gave up the manufacture of certain articles that could be secured from the white man, the Seminoles retained quite a few of the old skills. Many items of Seminole craftwork are intended for use in ceremonies, and are kept hidden from the eyes of the casual visitor. It may be of interest to enumerate some of the things made by the present-day Indians of Florida.

First there is the hut, usually thatched with palmetto leaves but occasionally shingled with slabs of cypress bark. The cooking hut is different from the dwellings, being floorless and having a fireplace in the center. There is also a more simple shelter constructed at hunting camps. Walkways on pilings are often built. Hammocks, low wooden stools, hide-stretching frames, and cooking grills are to be seen about Seminole encampments. Occasionally one encounters a coontie strainer; an elaborate affair of poles and deer skins, it is used to strain the poisonous juices from the otherwise edible roots of the coontie plant. Large wooden mortars and pestles are still made; the deep hole in

the mortar is burned out rapidly by means of a blowpipe. Wooden cups, mostly intended for sale, are likewise hollowed out by a burning and scraping technique. There are large and small sifters, curious tin graters, and a great variety of basketry. Most of the basketwork is intended for sale. The big wooden "sofki spoons" or ladles are interesting objects, and always well made. Some of the men know how to make silver ornaments with stamped or cut-out designs. Very large silver ornaments, such as turban bands, armlets, and crescent-shaped breast plates, are remembered, and it is said that a few are carefully preserved as heirlooms; but none is being made today. Ox carts were made within the memory of the older Seminoles, although they are not employed at the present time. Few new dug-outs are being made, but old ones in good condition are sometimes used on the canals of the Everglades. Dugouts are propelled by a push-pole; however, some were equipped with mast and sail, and a number of the Seminoles recall sailing on Lake Okeechobee and in the Ten Thousand Islands region. An unusual object of Seminole manufacture is a sugar cane grinder; it is an exact copy of the white man's grinder, but every part is carved from hard wood. The Seminole turtle spear is an ingenious device, much more effective for its purpose than the white man's gig. Even more ingenious is the "gopher puller"; it consists of a flexible vine with a wire hook at the end, and is used to extract the gopher tortoise (a big land turtle) from its burrow.

Bows and arrows are turned out, but only for the tourist trade; this is also true of beadwork, palmetto fiber dolls, toy spears and rattles, wooden tomahawks and knives, models of dugouts, carved and painted statuettes of a white heron, and many other items. Under the direction of a white man, a few of the Seminoles briefly revived the art of pottery manufacture; the vessels thus turned out were very attractive but, of course, quite unlike the original Seminole pottery.

Seminole clothing, with its elaborate patchwork design, is unique. Better-known items of Seminole costume include the man's dress, worn now by just a few of the elders; the man's shirt and a heavier jacket; the woman's dress, which sweeps the ground; the woman's vest; the woman's cape,

of some filmy or gauzy material; and children's dresses, often worn by small boys as well as girls. Some items of clothing, rarely seen by the white man, include the so-called "medicine man's coat" with ruffled epaulettes, and a plumed turban worn by some of the Indians on ceremonial occasions. An unusual item of dress is a frame of bark or of cypress, over which the women may arrange their hair to give a "hat brim" effect.

For their ceremonies the Indians make rattles of hafted coconut shells, and also of milk cans; women's dance rattles are of several box-turtle shells bound together. Seeds of the wild canna, which resemble buckshot, are always placed in the rattles. Other manufactures, used mostly at the Green Corn Dances, include a ceremonial scratcher, of needles inserted in wood or in the quill from a hawk's wing; tom-toms and water-drums; a leather ball, ball sticks, and score post, used in a game much like lacrosse; palmetto-leaf fans; a sweat - house; and cloth - wrapped reeds for the ceremonial procedure of "blowing into the medicine." At the Corn Dances, fires are kindled with an ancient flint-and-steel set, which the medicine man keeps with his other religious paraphernalia.

The Seminole elders recall other items now gone out of fashion: a cane flute used at the Corn Dances; high-topped moccasins of buckskin and sandals of alligator hide; tobacco sacks made from a pelican's pouch; beaded pouches and shoulder sashes; ear ornaments and finger rings; silver spangles that once decorated the women's capes; and waist-high leggins of fringed buckskin. A few of these objects have reached museums or private collections.

The foregoing list of Seminole manufactures is far from complete; many other items are, or until recently were, made by these Indians. Of course, the material possessions of the Seminoles likewise include a variety of things obtained from the white man. About almost every camp will be found pots and pans, kettles, pails, lard cans, chairs, children's toys, women's jewelry, men's neckerchiefs and neckerchief slides, boots and shoes, wire fencing, mosquito bars, blankets, hand - operated sewing machines, sewing kits, hammers, saws, hatchets, axes, knives, nails, shotguns, and ammunition.

Creek Indian cabin, (Upper) about 1790. Similar cabins were built by early Seminoles. (Lower) Present-day Seminole hut.

Use of F ... ood of the Seminoles

The Seminoles l. ... re, and utilize the local
flora and fauna in va ... ny plants and animals
are used by them for ... be pointed out subsequently. However, these ... nd on the plant king-
dom for many things o ... tenance. Their huts,
for instance, are commoni ... pond cypress logs and
poles, thatched with the fai ...aped leaves of the cabbage-
palm or of the smaller palmetto. Although board flooring
is now often used, some huts are floored with split logs of
the cabbage-palm. Sometimes, cabbage-palm logs provide
the hut's framework, also. Dugouts are always made from
the bald cypress, and push-poles from the smaller pond
cypress. "Sofki spoons" and other wooden items are gen-
arally of cypress, also. A tall pine sapling serves as a goal
post in the Seminole ball game. Ball sticks or racquets are
often made from bay wood, although sometimes improvised
from the midrib of a cabbage-palm leaf. Plumes of pine or
of bay branches decorate the corners of the ceremonial
structure on the Corn Dance grounds. Wire-grass is used in
basketwork. A large bamboo (not native to Florida) yields
fishing poles; and sections of this giant cane are made into

curios, such as tobacco pipes and small boxes. Hollow sections of cane are made into blowing tubes, useful when burning out a mortar or a wooden cup. Sifters are often made from strips of cane, neatly plaited. The milky latex of the strangler-fig is tapped, heated until it coagulates into rubber, and then used as chewing-gum. Coconut shells, with a few canna seeds therein, are mounted on wooden handles to make rattles. Hollow reeds are used by the medicine men to blow into the brews they mix at the Corn Dances. Palm fiber is used to make dolls. Fans made from palmetto leaves are carried during certain dances.

The Seminoles attribute medicinal properties to a number of plants; and indeed, many of these do contain medicinal ingredients. Two very important Seminole medicines, ginseng root and the bark of a certain species of willow, cannot be obtained in Florida, and so the Indians of that state obtain the plants from their brethren in Oklahoma. The angelica, a goosefoot, a mint, a false-indigo, a Florida elm, a boneset, a St. John's wort, bittersweet, and several other plants are included in the Seminole materia medica. During the Corn Dances, the old men often gather a plant they call "hot root"; an infusion therefrom is rubbed like liniment on aching joints.

Most Indian tribes of the Southeast made a ceremonial brew which white men called the "black drink." An emetic, purgative, and diuretic, it was drunk during the Corn Dance ceremonies as a rite of purification. Most of the tribes prepared their "black drink" from the cassine, a species of holly; and this seems to have been true of the early Seminoles. However, today other plants are used. In fact, there are at least three different "black drinks" among the present-day Seminoles. One of these is made from the button snake-root and another from the inner bark of the southern red willow. The third "black drink," a potent brew indeed, is made from roots of the southern red willow and of the button snake-root, as well as ginseng; the leaves of the red bay, the sweet bay, a pennyroyal, a blueberry, several wild grapes, the lizard's-tail plant, the southern red cedar, the mistletoe, and a small grass with whitish leaves; and from the entire plant of the rabbit-tobacco. There are a few other herbal ingredients beside

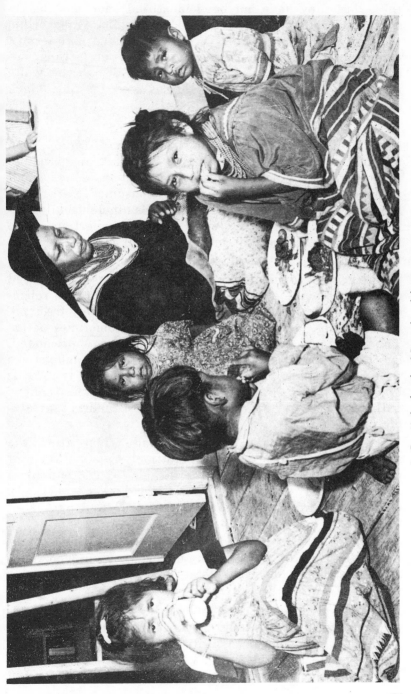

A Seminole family. Note the elaborate costumes.

these, but they have not been identified; nor has the resultant concoction been analyzed chemically. It is certain that this third "black drink" is rich in caffeine; and it must contain tannin, for it looks and tastes like very strong, bitter tea. As a matter of fact, the Seminoles call the white man's tea by the same name that is used for the "black drink".

FOOD OF THE SEMINOLES

The diet of the Seminoles is not very different from that of many rural white families in Florida. They eat quite a lot of meat, especially beef and venison. Much small game, such as squirrel and turkey, is consumed. Pork, froglegs, and turtle are also relished. The Seminole usually prefers his meat cut up in a stew. Fishes are important in the Indians' diet, and many kinds are caught and eaten.

Corn is much favored by the Seminoles, who roast it, or else grind it to make hominy grits. Corn meal is prepared and used to make cornbread. Biscuits and gravy are relished by the Seminoles. Pumpkins, sweet potatoes, Irish potatoes, beans, peas, and sugar cane are sometimes eaten. The tender bud of the cabbage palm, either raw or cooked, is often utilized. Guavas, oranges, limes, and bananas are frequently at hand about Seminole camps, and in the woods blueberries, wild grapes, plums, and blackberries can be gathered. The very sour wild oranges are rendered palatable by baking.

In past times, the Seminoles made flour from the starchy roots of the "coontie" plant and from the roots of the smilax vine, but today most of their flour is bought at stores. Canned fruit, coffee, sugar, bread, crackers, cakes, candy, cold drinks, and tinned meats are often purchased there, too.

The Seminoles usually drink water with their meals, but coffee is also favored. Many of the Seminole men relish a bottle of beer; however, a state law prohibits the sale or gift of any alcoholic beverage to a Seminole.

The Seminoles do not feel obliged to eat three meals a day, at set hours; rather, they eat when hungry, and do not expect everyone necessarily to become hungry at the same time. Usually the family gathers around the cook-fire in the early morning, and often again in the evening. But

Charlie Cypress with an albino opossum. Only a few old Seminole men
still wear the dress.

all during the day a pot of stew or of *sofki* (grits) may be kept on the fire for the Indians to dip into at regular intervals. Tidbits from the nearest store may also be eaten at odd hours. On a hunting trip, however, a Seminole may eat nothing from dawn to dark.

In past times, most of the cooking was done in one vessel, and a single, large, wooden *"sofki* spoon" was passed from hand to hand around a circle. However, today, many Seminoles own plenty of pans, pots, and dishes, and the *sofki* spoon may be used only to ladle out individual portions.

In a Seminole encampment, one or more of the huts is built especially to serve as a sort of "kitchen". The cooking hut differs from the other shelter in that it is only partially floored or sometimes entirely floorless. Thus a fire can be built on bare ground and yet under shelter. Food and utensils may be kept on the floored portion; pots and pans are often suspended from the rafters.

The Seminoles are divided into various "clans", and these clans must not eat together at ceremonial gatherings. Thus a member of the Wind Clan must not eat with a member of the Tiger Clan, nor the latter with any of the Otter Clan, etc. This rule is not especially binding on the men. but the women adhere to it rigidly, at least in public affairs. Therefore, when many Seminole families gather for a feast, six or more cooking fires must be built—one for each clan.

CHAPTER THIRTEEN

Changing Styles

Within our own culture, styles change rapidly. We have only to glance back through a family album to realize what a difference a half-century can make in the styles of clothing, hair-do, etc. With the Seminoles, too, styles have changed throughout the years.

Take, for example, the matter of dwellings. Many people are surprised to learn that the Indians of the Southeast, even in prehistoric times, did not live in "teepees" or "wigwams", but instead built very nice log cabins. These cabins differed from those of the whites in that there was no chimney, but a smoke-hole instead. Toward the latter 1700's, progressive tribes such as the Creeks also adopted the chimney and several other modifications introduced by the white man.

Fortunately, a picture of a Creek Indian cabin, drawn about 1790, has come down to us. This picture is reproduced on Page 58. It will be recalled that, in the latter 1700's, bands of Indians were breaking away from the Creek Confederacy and migrating southward, where they formed the nucleus of the Seminole tribe. Thus the drawing serves to illustrate the Seminole dwelling at its best, in early days of the tribe. Several other types of buildings were made by the Creeks and Seminoles at that time. The first Seminole settlements in Florida were called "towns" by contemporary writers who saw them, and the dwellings therein were termed "houses".

But the Seminole towns were constantly being burned down by the whites during the long years of struggle; and the Seminoles soon came to abandon the cabin and to erect instead a simple, thatched hut without walls. This style of dwelling, generally called a "chickee", may have been borrowed from the primitive Indian tribes who inhabited Florida before the coming of the Seminole. Alternatively, a knowledge of pole-and-thatch hut construction may have reached the Seminoles from the West Indies, through the agency of the Spanish Indians. At any rate, the Spanish Indians were living in "chickees" as early as 1824, when the other Seminoles were still building cabins.

Seminole clothing, too, has changed. The typical costume of a chief, about 120 years ago, is shown on Page 10. Here we see a fringed skirt, a pouch supported by a decorated shoulder strap, leggins, a plumed turban, silver armlets and wristlets, a silver head band, and a breast ornament of silver crescents. This sort of costume was worn by Osceola and his contemporaries at ceremonial gatherings. Needless to say, battle dress was much less elaborate; it consisted of a long skirt reaching almost to the knees, high leggins of heavy buckskin, moccasins, a shot pouch, a powder horn, and a knife.

As time went by, the life of the Seminoles became mostly a series of battles and guerrilla raids, and the fine costumes soon disappeared. Some people have suggested that, when hostilities ceased, the Seminole women had little left but scraps from which to make clothing, and so they sewed these together in decorative patterns to produce as attractive a garment as possible. This patch-work style then came to be the accepted thing. The story may have a little basis in truth, for the intricate patch-work costumes of the present-day Seminoles certainly originated within the last century.

66

Albert Billie wearing typical costume of younger Seminole men: pants, a gaudy jacket, and a "ten-gallon" hat.

There is a story current in Florida that some chief "condemned" the Seminole men to wear dresses because they didn't fight hard enough. This tale is untrue; at one time all the Seminole men, including the most savage fighters and the ablest leaders, wore skirts. Dresses were simply the characteristic costume adopted by the Seminoles, just as blankets or eagle-feather bonnets characterized some other tribes.

A few old Seminole men still wear a one-piece dress (see Page 63). Some wear a two-piece outfit of blouse and skirt, a more recent innovation. The younger men, however, wear pants, either with a white man's shirt or with a brightly colored jacket made by the Seminole women. Vests are popular with the tribe.

Women's costumes have changed less than the men's. Almost all the Seminole women wear a long, sweeping skirt and a thin cape (see Page 107). In past times, nothing was worn under the cape; but today a blouse is called for. Some of the older women, when not in public, wear a very short blouse that leaves the midriff exposed. This is an old style among the Seminoles, although quite a modern one for us! Some of the Seminole girls, mostly those living in or near the big cities, have abandoned all the Indian styles. Young boys may wear the old-time skirt, or may be given overalls or blue-jeans. Little girls wear sweeping dresses. Children's costumes appear in the photographs on Pages 69 and 71.

The old-time Seminole decorated pouch has been abandoned. A few silver ornaments have been handed down as family heirlooms, but are not worn. One or two old Seminoles still wear a turban, but most prefer "ten-gallon" cowboy hats (see Page 67). Plumes of the egret (a white heron) may be worn in the turban on ceremonial occasions.

In early times, a Seminole warrior had his hair shaved away except for a crest across the front and another down the crown. A few aged Seminoles today still wear this old-time "scalp-lock". Charlie Cypress, patriarch of the Silver Springs group, has most of his hair shaved away at regular intervals, leaving sometimes the traditional double crest, and sometimes a single crest across the front.

Seminole girls making dolls.

Two or three decades ago, almost every Seminole matron wore 25 or 30 pounds of beads, in string after string, about her neck. Some of the women still adhere to this custom, but most of the young girls wear only a few strings.

Seminole weapons and utensils have changed somewhat, also. Of course, the tribe had its beginning well within the historic period, and even in early times much equipment was procured from the white man. Aboriginal arts, such as weaving, pottery making, and the chipping of flint into tools and weapons, were unimportant when clothes, chinaware, and iron implements could be purchased from trading posts. Thus many of the old crafts disappeared at an early date.

The art of pottery manufacture was completely lost by the Seminoles, but recently a white man instructed some of the Indians in techniques of this craft. They were encouraged to duplicate the fine, decorated pots and bowls that prehistoric Indians of the Southeast had made. Under the man's direction, the old art was revived for a short while.

Even during the Seminole Wars, the Indians were mostly equipped with firearms, although the use of the bow and arrow was known. During the third Seminole uprising, when the tribe had been reduced to an impoverished remnant, the bow again became important, especially for hunting, since it was necessary to conserve ammunition. To make an arrow point, the Seminole rolled a thin piece of iron into a sharp cone, and inserted the arrow shaft into the cone's base. The present-day Seminole makes bows and arrows, but only to sell as curios; hunting is usually done with a shotgun. Some of the older Indians recall hunting with the bow and arrow in their earlier days.

Methods of transportation have changed greatly among the Seminoles. In the early days, travel was afoot or by horseback. Heavy loads were carried by ox-cart. As the Indians were pushed into the big swamps, dug-out boats

Almost every Seminole girl owns a sewing machine.

became more and more important. At one time the Seminoles made large dug-outs, equipped with mast and sail, for ocean navigation; and in these vessels they were able to reach Cuba and the Bahamas. Dug-outs up to 30 feet in length are still in use but few new ones are being made. Today some Seminoles own air-boats, and many have trucks or automobiles. Each year the state issues the "tribe" about 200 free auto license tags bearing the words "Seminole Indian." Some of the Indians prefer to buy the tags rather than accept free ones.

CHAPTER FOURTEEN

Songs and Ceremonies

The Seminole is rather secretive about his native songs, chants, and ceremonies; and is apt, when asked, to disclaim the existence of such. Thus many writers have been misled into stating that the old ceremonies have died out. This is far from the case. A few years ago, a worker from the Smithsonian Institute gained the confidence of Panther (also called Josie Billie), who was persuaded to make recordings of his tribal songs. He recorded no less than 75 songs including the Green Corn Dance and Hunting Dance, as well as the so-called Alligator, Catfish, Quail, Screech Owl, and other dances. This did not approach the number he knew. He also related tribal legends, singing the accompanying chants. These were in the Big Cypress or Hitchiti language. Another Seminole, Billie Stuart, recorded 125 songs in the Cow Creek or Muskogee language, and attributed 17 of these songs to the Calusa Indians who preceded the Seminoles in South Florida.

Among the Seminoles there are also women's songs, to be sung when performing household chores; lullabies to soothe the babies; group chants; medicine chants to accompany the treatment of the sick; and children's songs that are sung in connection with certain games. Many of these were recorded by the WPA Florida Writers' Project in 1940.

The best known ceremony of the present-day Seminoles is the so-called Green Corn Dance. This is an annual affair, conducted by the Big Cypress group usually in May or June; by the Trail-side Mikasuki generally around latter June or early July; and by the Cow Creek Seminoles between latter June and the middle of July. The date is set by the medicine man and his assistant. The Corn Dance lasts at least four days, sometimes longer. It varies in certain details, from group to group and from year to year. The usual procedure is about as follows:

The Indians begin to gather several days before the ceremony. Some help clean the dance grounds and repair the huts thereon, while others go hunting. At one time a grand hunt was staged just before the dance; but today, game being scarce, the medicine man and his assistants buy most of the food with the help of contributions from the participants. On the first day of the dance, early in the morning, the medicine man undergoes a ceremonial bath and then directs the preparations of the grounds. Men and boys gather wood for a dance fire; and in the afternoon there is a ball game in which the girls and young women play against the boys and young men. At night the fire is lit and several dances are staged. The second day is marked by feasting, and usually there is a barbecue. The men eat alone in a ceremonial hut called the "big house", while the women and children eat in clan camps nearby. On this day some man may go out to kill a white heron, the feathers of which will be used later on. In the afternoon another ball game may be held, and at night there are more dances. At midnight the men begin to fast. Early on the third day the medicine man and his assistants bathe ritually and bring out the sacred medicine bundles. Two "black drinks" are prepared, and partaken of by the men. Feathers of the white heron may be hung from poles, which are carried in the Feather Dance. This dance is staged twice in the morning and twice in the afternoon. About noon, court is held; medicine men and councilmen from other groups may be present at this time. These elders hear

74

Seminole dolls and manufactures. (Upper left) sugar cane press, entirely of wood. (Center) making sweetgrass baskets.

cases involving infractions of tribal laws, morals, and customs; and they pass judgment. Little is known of the punishments meted out; this aspect of Seminole culture is kept hidden from the white man. (According to some Christianized Seminoles, Indian justice is swift and certain.) In the afternoon there is another ball game, followed by dancing. At dusk the medicine man lights a fire, using a flint-and-steel which is kept in the medicine bundle. The contents of the bundle are displayed. Four ears of corn are placed by the medicine fire, one to each point of the compass. On the fire, the third "black drink"—the one of numerous ingredients—is prepared. While the concoction boils, dances are staged. The brew boils until midnight, when the ears of corn are placed in the pot. Then the drink is taken by the men, who soon purge themselves. The medicine man, his assistants, and a few others talk and tell stories until dawn, while all the other Indians continue dancing. Some years, a naming ceremony is held shortly after midnight; boys around 13 to 15 years old receive a new name, chosen by elders of their clan or by the medicine man. At dawn of the fourth day, the medicine man hides the sacred bundle, and then scratches the men and boys, using a small implement in which needles have been inserted. This ritual scratching is not severe; it is thought to insure future healthiness. In the morning the remains of the "black drink" are poured on heated stones in the sweat-house, and the men take an equivalent of a "Turkish bath." Then everyone bathes in cold water, and the long fast is broken. For the first time, the Seminoles eat of the new corn crop; for them a new year has begun.

There are at least 30 different dances that may be staged during the Seminoles' annual ceremony. Most of these are named for animals. In the Catfish Dance, the arms from the elbows make circles, in imitation of a catfish's fins. In the Alligator Dance the line of dancers resembles a writhing alligator. In the very striking Buffalo Dance, the medicine man pounds a small tom-tom as he dances; he paws the ground, snorts, and tosses his head like an angry buffalo bull. A rifle may be fired into the air at intervals during the Buffalo Dance. There is a Steal Partner dance, a well-liked social dance among the Seminole girls and boys. There is a Woodpecker Dance, a

Josie Billie, Seminole Baptist minister.

Screech Owl Dance, a Quail Dance, a Chicken Dance, a Feather Dance, and so on. Men, women, and children take part in all the dances except the Feather Dance, which is only for the men. Not all the dances are of religious import; some are purely for entertainment.

From time to time the Seminoles have held ceremonies other than the Corn Dance. These other ceremonies are remembered, but apparently have not been staged in the last few years. Until recently, there was a Hunting Dance held in the fall. It lasted about four nights, involving a hunt and a dance in which masks of cypress bark were worn. Canoe-building ceremonies have also been staged.

The Seminoles use few musical instruments in their songs and ceremonies. In the past, rattles were made from coconut and turtle shells; today tin cans are also used. Water-drums and tom-toms are made and used at the Green Corn Dance. The older Seminoles remember a cane flute that was played at the Dance, and a few of these instruments have reached museums; but the art of making and playing them has apparently died out. For many of the dances the women wear bunches of turtle-shell rattles bound to their legs.

Curiosity-seeking white people are not welcome at the Green Corn festival, and the Seminoles make an effort to keep them out. Before the Dance, the Indians are reticent about the date on which it is to be held, and, if directly questioned, will often declare that the ceremonies have already taken place. When the Seminoles gather for the affair, they customarily post a guard at the road leading to the ceremonial grounds; he attempts to halt intruders. However, white people who are especial friends of the Indians are invited to attend the dancing and feasting, and are excluded only from the trials conducted by the tribal "judges".

The Dania Seminoles no longer stage a Green Corn Dance, and in recent years they have not attended the Dances of the other tribal groups. Some of the Cow Creek Seminoles attend the Mikasuki festivals, but the reverse is rarely true.

CHAPTER FIFTEEN

Native Religion of the Seminoles

Some of the Seminoles have never adopted any Christian faith. This is not due to any lack of effort on the part of the missionaries, but to the Seminoles' antipathy toward the white man and all his ways. The older Indians, especially, adhere to the ancient tribal beliefs; some of them have even repudiated their brethren who have accepted the white man's creeds.

Probably no outsider understands the native Seminole religion very well. Only a brief outline of it, as gleaned from Mikasuki informants, can be given. Apparently the non-Christian Seminoles conceive of the existence of a "Great Spirit". It can not be said whether this concept is of aboriginal origin, or whether it results from white contact. Some of the Indians consider this spirit to be beneficent, others consider him impersonal. In addition, there are lesser spirits, some good and some bad. Certain Seminoles equate these lesser beings with the Christian angels and devils, respectively. The various spirits may influence the affairs of men; fortunately, they can be propitiated by offerings or by suitable prayers. Some of the spirits are thought to live in a sky-world above the earth, others in a subterranean world. All living creatures and many inanimate objects, including man-made ones, have spirits which are released when the creature dies or the object is broken. The souls of the dead eventually make their way to the spirit world, but for a time they may remain on earth as inimical ghosts; therefore it is best to abandon a camp where a death has taken place. The sun, moon, rainbow, and other manifestations of nature are somehow supernatural, either spirits or the work of spirits.

Much of the native Seminole religion centers around the so-called medicine bundles, mentioned in connect·on with the Green Corn Dance. These bundles contain bits of minerals, stones, various powders, snake fangs, bones, pieces of horn, and numerous dried herbs, as well as dance rattles and a flint-and-steel from which a ceremonial fire is lighted at the Corn Dance. The items are wrapped in buckskin, and the bundle is thought by the Indians to have great supernatural powers. According to Seminole belief, the original bundle was given to two medicine men by a mythical being, the adopted son of the Corn Mother. Smaller bundles of medicine were made up from the main one. Some of these were lost or went to Oklahoma during the Seminole Wars with parties or captives; at the end of the wars, just a few bundles remained in Florida. Three of these were accidentally destroyed in fires. At present there is one bundle for the Cow Creek Seminoles, one for the Mikasukis of Big Cypress Swamp, and six for the Mikasukis who live along the Tamiami Trail. The bundles are in the keeping of the medicine men, who guard them carefully. The keepers of the bundles preside at the Corn Dances; they also select and train their successors.

The Seminoles believe in the existence of a number of legendary creatures. These include mischievous little manlike dwarfs that live in the ground, and mythical serpents, of unusual size or abilities, that roam the swamps or hide in charms or talismans, which may help to bring good fortune and to ward off bad. They feel that there is a reality transcending ordinary existence, so that, under proper conditions, an animal might speak or a stone move.

At first it would seem that the Seminoles are beset by a multitude of beliefs and superstitions. But let us consider

80

A young Seminole girl.

for a moment the average "backwoods" white man in the South. He, too, believes in a Supreme Being, and a host of lesser spirits, the good angels and the bad devils. He believes that the souls of the dead make their way to a spirit world; but he also thinks that they may remain on earth as inimical ghosts, and nothing could persuade him to spend a night in a cemetery. He attributes great supernatural powers to the moon; he absolutely will not plant crops, geld stock, kill hogs, or undertake any important farm activity unless the moon is "right". He does not know what he means by "right" or how to tell when the moon is "right", and so he takes the word of some old man who, in his wisdom, solemnly pronounces that the moon will be "right" on certain nights. He also attaches a supernatural belief to the more unusual manifestations of nature, especially ball-lightning and will-o-the-wisps. He does not believe in mischievous little man-like dwarfs that live underground, but his great-grandmother believed in them and even set out bowls of milk to propitiate them. He does believe, with every fiber of his being, that the swamps and woods are inhabited by mythical serpents. He is actually belligerent in his insistence that the "hoop snake" exists; that it rolls like a hoop and has a stinger in its tail; and that his aunt died from the sting of one. He is sure, too, that there is a "tie-snake" that will tie a man's hands and then beat him to death; his father once killed one with a mowing machine, and so to question the existence of the "tie-snake" is to impugn his father's veracity. He puts faith in many charms and talismans: a rabbit's foot, a lucky buck-eye, a "beezle-stone" supposedly from the heart of a deer, or a hair-ball procured from the local Negroes. He would never be found without a pair of "High John the Conqueror" roots, which he bought from a mail-order house; of course he needed two, one to bring good fortune and the other to ward off evil. He is sure that some creatures possess mystic powers. When the beautiful little ground-dove calls near the house, he believes it presages a death in the family. He is quite convinced that the "joint-snake" can break into pieces and later reassemble; he will tell you in all sincerity that no power on earth can prevent this reassembling. He thinks that the dainty little hummingbird is very poisonous, and is sure that the "pilot snake" guides the rattlesnake to a suitable den each winter. Those gauzy-winged insects, the dragon-flies, he calls "snake-doctors", and insists that they tend injured snakes and sew up their wounds. He also is certain that "snake-doctors" will sew up your lips and ears, and that "earwigs" will crawl into your ear whnever they get a chance. He believes that the yellow-billed cuckoo, which he calls "rain-crow", can infallibly predict rain. He holds fast to dozens of other superstitions which need not be recounted here. We have little cause to scoff at the Seminoles' beliefs, which are no more fantastic than those held by many thousands of rural white southerners.

In the Seminole mind there is no clear separation beween religion and medicine. Many illnesses are thought to be produced by spirits, or by foreign objects which make their way into the system in some mysterious manner. The treatment of disease includes not only real therapeutic measures but also appropriate rituals or incantations. Therefore, the Seminoles who know the most about religious matters are also called in to treat the sick and injured. The Indians call these wise men "doctors"; there are several such medicine-men among the Florida Seminoles today. It is interesting to note that one of the best-known present-day Seminole Baptist ministers was, in his youth, a leading medicine-man, famed for his knowledge of herbal remedies and the rituals that accompany their use.

Most Seminoles who die are buried by their own people in the swamps or woods. Among the Cow Creek group the body is generally but not invariably placed in the ground. Among the Mikasuki the body usually is not interred, but placed in a coffin of planks or split logs which is left on the surface of the ground at some remote spot. A small thatched shelter is built over the coffin. Some of the possessions of the deceased are generally placed in the coffin with him. Among the Mikasuki (but not apparently among the Cow Creek), each item of possession is deliberately broken before it is placed with the dead. Tin pans are bent double, pots are flattened, pipe-stems are snapped, chinaware is chipped, even valuable objects such as rifles or shotguns are broken before being placed with the body.

This is done in the belief that breaking releases the "spirit" of the article, which will then accompany the deceased to the Hereafter. The custom is an ancient one, and was practiced centuries ago by prehistoric Indians in the Southeast and elsewhere. The Seminoles also put food and drink, in unbroken containers, outside the coffin. The body is placed with the feet to the east. Every evening for four days a fire is built near each end of the coffin.

In recent years some Seminoles have been buried at the government cemetery on the Dania Reservation. Most of these burials have been presided over by missionaries to the Seminoles. In addition, Deaconess Harriett M. Bedell, of the Glade Cross Episcopal Mission, has provided a cemetery for the Trail-side Seminoles at Everglades, Florida.

CHAPTER SIXTEEN

Missionary Activities Among the Seminoles

Until recently, most of the Seminoles adhered to their own tribal beliefs. This should not be surprising. Until the last few years, the Seminoles could expect nothing but treachery and oppression from the white man. Even today they are exposed, at times, to what they consider (and often is) unwarranted interference. They could scarcely be expected to readily embrace the religion of the people whom they have reason to mistrust. Nevertheless, just in the last decade a number of Seminoles have turned to Christianity, as a result of heavy pressure from missionaries and other agencies. The reservation Indians, of course, were the ones exposed to the most proselytizing; and to-day most of the Seminoles on the Dania Reservation, a majority of those on the Big Cypress Reservation, and some of those on the Brighton Reservation are Christians. The non-reservation Seminoles, living mostly along the Tamiami Trail, with but few exceptions have not accepted any Christian faith. As more than half of the Florida Seminoles do not live on reservations, it is correct to say that Christian Seminoles are still in the minority.

The methods of some missionaries, at least in the past, have sometimes been open to criticism; even leading churchmen admit this. The Reverend Mr. Lucien Spencer, Seminole Agent from 1913 until his death in 1930, was dean of the Episcopal Cathedral in Orlando before he entered the Indian Service, so he could scarcely be accused of prejudice against the church. He wrote as follows: "During the entire 24 years of my association with the Florida Seminoles I have never known of the case of a missionary working among them whose influence was not decidedly harmful. The Indian is naturally a very religious person and the detrimental effect of the missionary comes from the fact that they do not try to build up and enlarge the Indian's belief but proceed to destroy what religion he has and then leave the field without giving anything in return. It is an indisputable fact that in every instance the Indian shows a lower standard of honesty and morality after coming in contact with the missionary." Spencer's opinions were quoted by Roy Nash, U.S. Commissioner, who made an investigation of Seminole living conditions in 1930. It must be emphasized that these opinions were expressed more than 20 years ago, and had no reference to present-day missionaries, some of whom have remedied the conditions that so concerned Spencer and Nash.

From the Fort Lauderdale News, October 8, 1949: "A . . . missionary to the Seminole Indian camp at Dania . . . was suspended as a result of the whipping he idministered to three Seminole girls several weeks ago after they had allegedly attended a dance in Ft. Lauderdale in company of his son . . . (The missionary) admitted whipping the girls (ages 23, 17, and 19) . . . The whipping was administered with an electric light cord folded to four thicknesses, according to an affidavit signed by the girls . . . The (missionary) has been called a "disturbing influence" at the reservation by (the) Seminole Indian superintendent, who . . . charged (the missionary) with "taking over" the sale of Indian novelties and dresses made by the Seminoles, and with exploiting the Indians to his own profit." The article further comments: "(The missionary) has stated that he . . . will hold Sunday church services . . . across the . . . highway from the reservation, whether the mission board wants it or not." Such an episode, which

A gallery of Seminole portraits. The kindly humor of aged Charlie Cypress contrasts with the quizzical brightness of the Seminole children, and the stern dignity of Tom Tiger with the modesty of the girls grinding corn.

is by no means an isolated one, is most deplorable, for it arouses resentment among the Indians, and tends to obscure the good works accomplished by some missionaries.

But there is a bright side to the picture. Some missionaries have not only been true friends of the Seminoles, but have combined with their enthusiasm a keen wisdom, discretion, and understanding. No better illustration of this could be found than in the work of Deaconess Harriet M. Bedell of the Glade Cross Episcopal Mission at Everglades, Florida. Her activities have been a direct refutation of the criticisms leveled by Spencer. Deaconess Bedell has worked with the Indians of the western United States, among remote Alaskan tribes on the Arctic Circle, and—for 17 years—with the Seminoles of Florida. Knowing that the spread of Christianity among Indians has been slowed by the squabbling of different religious denominations, she made no effort to alter the beliefs of the reservation Seminoles, who had come under Baptist influence. Instead, she devoted her attention to the Indians along the Tamiami Trail from Fort Myers to Miami, and to those families living far back in the swamps. At first—like all white strangers—she was met only with stolid indifference; but few people could resist Deaconess Bedell's gracious ways for long, and eventually many of the Indians became her firm friends. She visited the remotest camps, traveling by car, afoot, and by Seminole dug-out; and soon the Indians began coming to her for help and advice in all sorts of matters.

At Everglades, Deaconess Bedell prepared a mission village where visiting Seminoles could stay when they came to shop or to see the doctor. Then, with the help of friends, she leased an abandoned village on the Tamiami Trail, and had the settlement rebuilt. A large assembly "chickee", a cooking hut, several family dwellings, and a bath house were erected there, and sanitary conveniences were installed. The two villages opened many opportunities for mission work, and provided places where the Indians could assemble for group activities, Christmas celebrations, and friendly festivals.

Deaconess Bedell established an account for the Seminoles at a store near the mission; but she insisted that

88

they bring in items of handicraft in exchange for credit. Next she sought and found a market for the Indians' craftwork, and then arranged with the Seminoles a schedule of prices. She told the Indians that she would sell for them only those items of high quality, made in the traditional Seminole styles. Today the Seminoles bring the best and most representative items of their handicraft to Deaconess Bedell, who soon locates a buyer. It would be better to say that the buyers come to Deaconess Bedell; even professional anthropologists, seeking to round out their collections of genuine Indian craftwork, make their way to Glade Cross Mission. The project not only brings financial aid to the Seminoles, but also makes them feel that their arts and crafts are truly worthwhile.

Some missionaries among non-Christian peoples have tried to crush all native culture—arts, crafts, languages, songs, games, festivals, styles of clothing, methods of livelihood. Nothing is more pathetic than the maladjusted remnant of a once-happy people whose entire cultural tradition has been scorned, scoffed at, and derided into oblivion. Deaconess Bedell, well grounded in psychology, knows this, and so she helps the Indians to keep their dignity and self-respect, and makes them feel that their own secular ways and customs are commendable.

Although many religious denominations have concerned themselves with the Seminoles, only two have made any noticeable headway: the Episcopal among the Trail-side Indians, and the Baptist on the reservations. There are now Baptist churches on the Dania and Big Cypress reservations. In recent times, most of the Baptist ministers and missionaries have been Indians, either Florida Seminoles or Creeks and Seminoles from the Oklahoma reservations.

From the Lakeland Ledger, September 29, 1946: "Five Seminole Indians . . . have begun religious training in Lakeland so they may return to the Everglades to preach and teach the Christian faith. Junior Buster, Josie Billie, Barfield Johns, Billie Osceola, and Sam Tommie are first-year students at the Florida Baptist Institute, which is conducted on a high school level for the training of future pastors as well as laymen. Their appearance here for the school's opening . . . marked a sharp break with Seminole tradition, for this proud tribe, technically still at war with the United States, has long been aloof from white men . . . The Institute has started courses in reading, writing, elementary speech, and singing, since the new students came with no formal education and little command of English . . . As they make progress in these elementary subjects, the Indians will begin courses in advanced English, mathematics, science, history, geography, public speaking, the Bible, and Bible-related subjects, which are part of the three-year curriculum . . . " It may be added that today three of these Indians are Baptist ministers.

CHAPTER SEVENTEEN

Marriage, Divorce and Education

Seminole morality is quite good. The code of sexual behavior is rigid, and although there has been some lowering of standards as a result of white contacts, even the most strait-laced missionaries have found little to complain of in this direction.

The average Seminole is generous to his acquaintances, kindly and sympathetic to those in need, polite in his behavior, honest in his dealings, stoic in the face of adversity, and dependable in an emergency.

The most widespread vice among the Seminoles is intemperance. Few peoples are more repressed and inhibited than the Seminoles, who rarely even raise their voices or make bold gestures. They find little opportunity for emotional outlet except through intoxication. A psychologist once described the gaudy Seminole costumes as "a strong man's reaction against monotony", and the same characterization might be applied to the Indians' occasional drunkenness. Certainly nothing is more monotonous than the Seminole country, which often depresses even casual visitors; and nothing is more barren of amusement than the every-day existence of these Indians. In 1930, Roy Nash, U.S. Commissioner, wrote about the Seminoles' opportunity for entertainment in the little white communities of the Everglades: "Not even a moving-picture show. Where the very pinnacle of excitement is attained by peeping in the door of the pool-room or watching country gawks shuffle through the figures of a quadrille to the accompaniment of a mouth organ and a discordant fiddle . . . What else is there to do except get drunk . . .?" The situation is about the same today.

Under the influence of even a little alcohol, the Seminole's character completely alters. He becomes loud, talkative, offensive; soon he may become violent. The few Seminoles who have broken the white man's laws have almost always been inebriated.

Federal law prohibits the sale or gift of any alcoholic beverage to a Seminole. Nevertheless the Indians procure whiskey, for the Everglades swarm with bootleggers eager to peddle their "rot-gut" to the Seminoles, at exorbitant prices. The Indians also pay the local Negroes to buy whiskey and beer for them. A certain amount of money is left in a place previously agreed on, usually in the thick grass beside the trail leading to a Seminole village. A Negro later picks up the money, buys the desired beverage, and leaves it in the grass. Most of the Seminoles fear to ask white men to aid them in these illegal transactions.

Some Indians who cannot procure alcohol have adopted the curious custom of "gasoline sniffing". They take a small can of gasoline, dip a cloth into it, and inhale the fumes until they become stupefied. Apparently the practice is somewhat habit-forming. It would also seem to be illegal, for the Fort Myers News-Press of August 29, 1946, reported that two Seminoles were arrested for such "sniffing". This practice, it may be mentioned, was learned by the Indians from the white men; it is frequently resorted to in slums and "hobo jungles" by alcoholics and dope-addicts who are unable to procure the more usual intoxicants and narcotics.

It is evident that the Seminoles are badly in need of amusements; of recreation centers where they could gather

A Seminole family. Note the elaborate costumes.

for sports, games, moving-pictures, and harmless fun; of sights other than saw-grass marsh under a blazing sky.

The Florida Seminoles rarely use the white man's churches or courts for marriage or divorce. These ceremonies are carried on in the old way, according to tribal law and custom. Federal law recognizes these "Indian Custom" marriages and divorces as legal.

A Seminole couple was married by civil authorities in 1926, and another in 1928. In 1948 a Baptist Church was opened on the Big Cypress Reservation, and the following year a young Seminole couple was married there strictly in the white man's fashion. This event received much attention from local newspapers, most of which stated incorrectly that a Seminole couple had never before been married in other than native style.

In past times, a Seminole man was permitted and in fact expected to have two wives. Usually the wives were sisters or at least close relatives of each other, although this was not invariably the case. However, the custom of polygamy slowly died out, seemingly of its own accord. Very likely, the Seminole men found it impossible to support two wives, what with the increasing shortage of wild game and the difficulty of making a living. Today polygamy has disappeared entirely, except in the case of one very elderly man who still has two wives. This individual is not Indian by race, being a descendant of the Seminole Negroes.

Contrary to popular belief in Florida, Seminole law does not absolutely prohibit intermarriage with the whites. Three Seminole men today have white wives, and one Seminole woman has a white husband. As mentioned previously, the Seminoles are divided into clans. Thus there are the Panther, Wildcat, Bird, Otter, Wind, Wolf, Snake, and Town Clans, among others. A Seminole is expected to marry outside his or her own clan. Descent is reckoned in the female line and so the children are born into the mother's clan, not the father's. In consequence of this arrangement, young Seminoles are instructed in many matters not by their fathers but by their maternal uncles. The avuncular relationship among the Seminoles is thus more important than with us. Also, certain clans are said to stand

94

in an "uncle-nephew" relationship to each other. For example, Panther Clan is "uncle" of the Wildcat Clan; the Wind Clan is "uncle" of the Bird Clan. Two clans, so related, are called a phratry in anthropological parlance. The Seminoles consider it desirable to marry not only outside the clan but also outside the phratry. If a Cow Creek Seminole marries a Mikasuki, as sometimes happens, the children are born into the mother's "tribe" or group, and are taught to speak the mother's language.

WOMEN IN SEMINOLE SOCIETY

Many white people think that "Indian women did all the work while the men just hunted and fished." This is an erroneous interpretation of the Indian way of life. Let us consider the position of women in Seminole society. Among the Seminoles, the woman, not the man, might be considered the real family head. True, she sits in the background when the men gather, saying little and working busily—but she owns most of the property, the hut, the utensils, the cattle. When a Seminole man says, "I am going home," he means he is going to his wife's home or to his mother's home, depending on whether he is married or not. Descent and inheritance are reckoned through the female side of the family; and when a couple gets married, the man goes to his bride's hut to live. The education of children is mostly in the hands of the mother and her brothers.

These customs were rigidly adhered to until very recent times, when increasing contact with the whites brought about some changes. Most white men, ignorant of Seminole social organization, insisted on dealing with the "man of the house" in business matters, persisted in calling Seminole children by their father's surname, and in general acted as though the Seminole customs were identical with their own. Thus many Seminole families have accepted the white man's way, out of sheer necessity; but nevertheless the aboriginal system still exists.

As far as actual work is concerned, the Seminole women, past or present, were responsible for the housework, the cooking, and the care of smaller children; while to the men fell the tasks of providing food, training the older boys, defending the household against enemies, and performing those chores requiring much physical strength. Matters of state were left to the men, while domestic affairs were pretty much up to the women. "Stag parties", "hen parties", and mixed gatherings were held. In short, the Seminole way at least in its broader outlines, was and is not very different from our own.

EDUCATION

At the present time, no effort is made to force the Seminoles into sending their children to school. Only in the last few years have the Indians shown much voluntary interest in formal education. Florida law stated that only white children may attend the white schools. This law was intended to segregate Negroes and whites, and was not aimed at the Seminoles. Therefore the Seminole children have been encouraged by the Indian Agency to attend white schools where possible. Teachers, local boards of education, and the parents of white children have favored the admission of the young Indians into the public schools. Thus, about 30 little Seminoles go to school in Dania, 55 in Okeechobee, 8 in Miami, 5 in Ocala, and 5 in Everglades. The Indians have refused to attend Negro schools.

The federal government maintains a school on the Brighton Reservation, and another at the Big Cypress Reservation. The latter was forced to close for several years on account of inadequate roads and the lack of a teacher. It was opened in 1956, however, and had about 27 pupils.

Seminole children wishing advanced training and education may attend the government boarding school on the Cherokee Reservation in North Carolina. This school, in addition to elementary courses of study, has a regular four-year high school curriculum, including vocational training. Twenty - odd Seminole youths have been enrolled there yearly, in recent times. At the present writing, no Florida Seminole is a college graduate; seven have completed high school, and others are in attendance. About 22 older students are attending Sequoia Vocational School in Oklahoma.

Since 1951, county truant officers have attempted to keep some check on Seminole school attendance in South Florida.

CHAPTER EIGHTEEN

Citizenship and Legal Status

In 1924 a federal law was passed declaring that all Indians born in the United States are citizens of that nation and of the state in which they reside. Theoretically this included the Florida Seminoles. In practice, the decree made little difference to these Indians, who did not even "recognize" the United States government. The Seminole can vote and hold public office, if he should-ever want to. (As a matter of fact a few Seminoles have voted each year in recent times.) He can buy and own land, if he should ever have the money. He can own personal property and execute valid contracts. He must obey the state hunting and fishing laws except when on federal lands. Although supposedly a citizen, he is also a "ward of the government", and federal law has forbidden the sale of alcoholic beverages to him. At the present writing, the federal government has relaxed this regulation and plans to remove all Indians from the "wards of the government" category. State law still prohibits sale of alcoholic beverages to the Seminoles.

Seminoles rarely break the white man's laws. When they do, they are treated with leniency. White offenders against the Seminoles are usually treated firmly. It may be said that the courts take cognizance of the Seminole's anomalous positions and status, and strive to protect his legal rights in individual cases. Infractions of Seminole law are handled by the tribal elders at the Green Corn Dance, as mentioned previously.

In 1946, many South Florida newspapers blatantly proclaimed that the Seminole tribal council had condemned to death a young Indian maiden because she had a white lover. This supposed incident was a hoax, perpetrated for the sake of notoriety by certain individuals who exhibited Seminoles as a tourist attraction. The hoax reached absurd proportions, and sheriffs were even sent into the Everglades to question the bewildered Indians. The Miami Herald, a progressive newspaper and one much interested in the Seminoles' welfare, exposed the fraud.

Actually, the Seminole tribal councils last administered the death penalty in 1938. The executioners were arraigned in the white man's court, but the incident was declared "justifiable homicide" and the case was dismissed. The Florida Seminoles are perhaps the only group of people in this country that has been allowed to inflict capital punishment.

Special mention should be made of the work of the Seminole Indian Agency, now located at Dania, Florida. Indian Agents and their staffs have seldom been given to publicity-seeking, and the average person has little knowledge of their important work. It therefore seems desirable to present, first, a few remarks about Agents in general.

An Indian Agent is a representative of the federal government in its dealings with those Indians under the Agent's jurisdiction. He might be called the head of a great family whose members look to him for aid and protection. The Agency is concerned with the feeding, clothing, and sheltering of the Indians; with the maintenance of law and order; with the care of the sick, aged, or helpless; and with the providing of education. One might summarize by saying that the goals of the Agency are to advance the welfare of the Indians and to bring them to a point where they are capable of self-support.

Any Agent's office is apt to be a sort of clearing-house where Indians can air their grievances against trespassing whites; where problems of domestic relations can be worked out; where squabbles can be adjudicated. The Agent must listen, also, to the plaints of bigoted white men who would grant the Indians no rights whatsoever; must deal with the "do-gooders" and professional friends of the Indians who are well-meaning but often woefully ignorant of actual facts; must answer the queries of newspaper reporters, visiting tourists, and would-be authors; must stand as a buffer between warring church factions each anxious to convert the Indians in its own way and no other. In addition, the Agent must travel widely, inspecting the living conditions of the Indians and checking on the work of his subordinates; he must submit various reports and comply with the government's proverbial "red tape" regulations; and he must carry out orders handed down to him from Washington, D.C.

The Seminole Agency is faced with an unusual situation, for more than half of the Indians under its jurisdiction do not live on reservations, but maintain an independent existence in the swamps and along the Tamiami Trail. Furthermore, the Florida Seminoles, to a greater extent than most other Indians in this country, have kept alive the bitter memories of war, and still retain considerable antipathy toward the white man and his ways.

Contrary to popular opinion, reservation Indians in this country, regardless of tribe, do not live off government bounty; the allocation of supplies to the Indians is in payment of debts incurred by the federal government when it purchased lands from the tribes who were recognized as legal owners. The Florida Seminoles, however, reached no very definite business agreement with the government. An uninformed person might criticize the Agency because it did not distribute blankets to all the Seminoles, when in actual practice the federal government might not authorize or provide for such a distribution.

The author has previously discussed the work of the Seminole Indian Agency in providing schools for the Indians on the reservations, in encouraging the attendance of Seminole children at public schools, in supervising the important cattle-raising projects, in locating jobs for the Indians, and in finding a market for craftwork. The Agency also carries out a program of medical and dental care in the camps and on the reservations.

The Seminole road project is another interesting activity of the Agency. Under the direction of white engineers, the Indians have built many miles of roads in or near the reservations. With considerable pride in the Indians' achievements, the Agency announced in 1951 that the Seminoles had constructed a good road from State Highway No. 8C to the Big Cypress Reservation, across 40-odd miles of swamp. All the road-building machinery used in this project was operated by Seminoles, some of whom qualified themselves for subsequent jobs as operators of heavy equipment.

The Agency gives every assistance to those Indians who wish to qualify for Old Age, Aid to Dependent, or Blind Aid grants, which are available from the Florida State Welfare Department.

Just recently, the Florida Seminole Agency was brought under the headquarters supervising Seminole affairs on the Oklahoma reservation. The various Indian Agencies are directed by the Office of Indian Affairs, a branch of the United States Department of the Interior.

The current Seminole Indian Agent is Mr. Kenneth Marmon, who has worked with and for the Florida Seminoles since 1942. In addition to his other duties, Mr. Marmon has prepared two interesting articles on the Seminoles, both of them characteristically unsigned except as a contribution from the Agency. The first of these (listed in the bibliography as Anonymous, 1948) is a short, popular account of the Seminoles. The second (Anonymous, 1951) is a highly important summary of the present economic conditions of the Indians, and contains some recommendations which will interest those who are concerned with the Seminoles' welfare.

CHAPTER NINETEEN

Health, Population and Physical Anthropology

Fiction writers are fond of portraying swamps as deadly and disease-filled places. Actually, the crowded cities are much more unhealthful. The Seminoles live in the swampiest region of the United States, yet they are the healthiest of all Indian tribes in this country. This is almost surely due to the fact that they are a free people, living a natural life that is suited to their needs. They are in the open air at all times of day and night; they get a large amount of physical exercise; and almost every family is more or less isolated from its neighbors. People who are concerned with the welfare of the American Indians should take careful note of the fact that Florida Seminoles who live in the old way are far healthier than other Indians who have been forced into a manner of life to which they are not well adapted.

Like the rural whites in many parts of the South, the Seminoles contract malaria and hookworm. Beyond these two ills, disease is rare among the Florida Indians. Tuberculosis, trachoma, typhoid fever, dysentery, smallpox, measles, diptheria, mumps, scarlet fever, cerebrospinal meningitis, whooping-cough, cancer — such ailments have been relatively uncommon or even completely unknown among the Seminoles, in spite of the fact that the first two are scourges of Indians on the western reservations. Venereal diseases were virtually lacking among the Seminoles until the last quarter-century, and at present the rate of infection is lower than that in many white communities.

Although the Seminoles are unusually healthy, they often have poor teeth. Cavities, caries, and pyorrhea are common among the tribe. Some authorities attribute this to the fact that the Seminoles' diet consists mostly of meat and starches, with little milk and but few fresh vegetables. Lack of knowledge of oral hygiene is no doubt a contributing factor.

Medical work among the Seminoles has been hindered by the difficulty and expense of reaching these scattered swamp-dwellers, and by limited health appropriations. At the present time, one public health field nurse is expected to attend to the needs of more than 900 Seminoles, scattered over several thousand square miles of swamp. The nurse carries out a general health program, including dental care, in the camps and on the reservations.

There are no government hospitals for Seminoles, and no contract doctors. The Indians are generally accepted at any of four hospitals in South Florida. Occasionally there is an emergency case in which the Indian must be taken to a hospital that has not been designated by the government to accept Seminoles. This always poses a problem for payment. Some Seminoles pay their own medical costs, while an increasing number of them have been requesting medical or dental aid from the government.

Most expectant Seminole women now request hospitilization. Few babies are born in the camps, and so infant mortality is lower now than in the past.

Unfortunately, as the Seminoles associate with white people more and more, they contract the white man's diseases. The Indian children, in particular, contract various ailments from their white classmates, and then spread these disorders among the Indian families. Just in the last few years, chicken pox, measles, and whooping cough

A group of Seminoles. Note hair-do of woman at left, and framework of hut in backgrround.

have made their appearance. In 1949 the Seminoles, and especially the children, were swept by what many newspapers called a "mysterious malady". Seminole matrons, tearful and frightened, brought feverish children to local doctors and hospitals. The disease proved to be the familiar "strep throat"; and it soon yielded to medical treatment. In 1951 a severe epidemic of mumps swept the Big Cypress Reservation, hospitalizing many Indians. It is safe to predict that the Seminoles will become more and more disease-ridden as they abandon the swamps and become a part of civilized communities.

Many Seminole families still request the services of a native "medicine man", several of whom exist today. Josie Billie, Charlie Cypress, the late Doctor Tiger, and a few other elderly Indians have been much respected for their medical lore, and have often been called in even by the most educated Seminoles. The Seminole shaman relies on a number of herbs, most of which actually do contain medicinal ingredients, and which are used in our own pharmocopeia. He accompanies the use of herbal potions with lengthy chants, which are actually prayers. In addition, he sometimes practices blood-letting, making a hole in the patient's skin and sucking out the blood. Like many white physicians, the Seminole doctor knows that the patient must be impressed with the treatment, and must be put in the confident frame of mind that will facilitate recovery. Therefore the shaman often cleverly pretends to suck from the wound a bit of stone, a sharpened bone, a lizard, a beetle, or some other foreign object whose presence is supposed to have produced the patient's disorder. A favorite trick of the Seminole medicine man is to conceal in the mouth a dye; and when the patient's blood is sucked out and spat forth on the ground, it is a poisonous-looking black in color. This bit of charlatanry not only deceives the Indians; it has deeply impressed occasional white on-lookers as well. For his services the shaman usually receives cash, about $2.50 for the average case.

POPULATION

Around 1820, when the Seminole tribe was at its peak in numbers, it consisted of about 5,000 individuals. But a great many Seminoles submitted to removal, others were

Charlie Cypress beginning a dugout canoe. It will be carved in one piece from the cypress log. Charlie's dugouts are on display at Silver Springs and elsewhere in the state.

killed or captured, and a few fled to the Bahamas. Thus, by the end of the third Seminole War in 1858, the best contemporary estimates indicated less than 200 Indians left in Florida. Present-day anthropologists believe the number was closer to 300. In 1880, a census of the tribe showed only 208 Seminoles in the state; no doubt the actual population was slightly greater. The census of 1900 revealed 358. In 1908 the number had dropped to 275, for some unexplained reason. The Reverend Mr. Lucien Spencer, Seminole Agent from 1913 to 1930, kept a good record of the population, which increased greatly during that period. In 1930 there were 578 Seminoles in Florida, according to Mr. Spencer's tabulation. This figure agrees well enough with the findings of Nash, U.S. Commissioner who investigated the Seminoles of that time, and with the Indians' own estimate of their number in that year.

The census of 1940 turned in a figure of 590. By 1948 the number stood at 751. In September, 1951, there were 823 Seminoles in Florida. Of these, 425 were females and 389 males; 322 individuals were under 18 years of age. About 295 of the total population were the Muskogee-speaking "Cow Creek Seminoles", while the remainder were Mikasukis. In January, 1956, there were 945 Seminoles in Florida and by 1965 more than 1,500 Seminoles were counted. Obviously the Seminoles are not a "dying race"; they are increasing very rapidly.

In recent decades there has been very little intermarriage between the Seminole and any other race. The Seminoles are increasing rapidly and are maintaining their racial stock. This is quite contrary to the predictions of a generations ago, when it was thought that these Indians would either die out or be absorbed into other races. In September, 1951, about 728 of the 823 Seminoles were full-blooded Indians, according to the tabulations of the Indian Agency. The ratio has not changed significantly since.

PHYSICAL CHARACTERISTICS OF THE SEMINOLES

The ancestors of the American Indians reached this country many centuries ago, coming from Asia by way of the Bering Strait. Through this portal came peoples of different racial stocks, but predominant were the Mongo-

Mary and David Billie with a tame bear cub, at Silver Springs.

loids—the Eastern Asiatics with yellowish-brown skins. Thus, today, the American Indian is essentially Mongoloid, although with certain typical characteristics.

The Florida Seminole men, as a rule, are rather tall for Indians, and of good and symmetric development. The women are of medium height, tending toward stoutness in middle-age. The head is broad and round in both sexes. The face is broad, with high and prominent cheek-bones. The forehead is well developed, fairly broad and high. The nose is usually straight, sometimes high and arched, with moderately wide nostrils. The ear is small and often lobeless. The mouth is of medium width or more, the lips thin or of medium thickness. The jaws and teeth are usually large and strong. A "Mongoloid fold" of the eye is often present, and is more conspicuous in small children than in adults. The iris of the eye is generally dark brown, sometimes black. The hair of the head is thick, straight or wavy, black to dark brown or reddish-brown in color, fine to coarse in texture. The hair does not turn gray until very late in life, and becomes white only in extreme old age. Baldness never develops except among a few Indians with an admixture of white blood. Facial hair is sparse, but some old men sport mustaches. A small goatee was occasionally worn in past times. Body hair is very scanty. The skin color ranges from a yellowish-brown to a medium brown.

About 90% of the Florida Seminoles are listed as full-bloods. The remaining individuals show some white or Negro admixture. The white blood crept into the Seminole population very recently, while practically all the Negro admixture took place during the Seminole Wars, when runaway slaves fought side by side with the Indians against a common enemy.

CHAPTER TWENTY

Seminole Languages

As mentioned previously, the Seminoles were a group of composite origin, and even today two different languages exist among them. The Indians on the Brighton Reservation, and those living to the north of Lake Okeechobee, speak what is called Muskogee. The Indians on the Big Cypress, State, and Dania Reservations, and those living along the Tamiami Trail, speak a variant of Hitchiti; this variant is sometimes called Mikasuki. Muskogee and Hitchiti, although related languages, are mutually unintelligible.

Roughly, two-thirds of the Seminoles in Florida speak the Mikasuki language, but the several thousand Seminoles on the western reservation in Oklahoma speak only Muskogee. Thus the language generally called "Seminole" is Muskogee. It is also spoken by several thousand Creek Indians now in Oklahoma. All the variants of Hitchiti have died out, except the Mikasuki tongue that is spoken in Florida. A Seminole from the Brighton Reservation in Florida could not speak with a Seminole from the Big Cypress Reservation about 50 miles away, yet could converse readily with a Creek Indian, a member of an "enemy" tribe.

Both Muskogee and Hitchiti have relatively large vocabularies, and are very complex and difficult, full of idioms and constructions that seem strange to us. If one learned the entire Seminole vocabulary, one still could not speak the language, for the method of stringing words together into sentences is quite different from ours. In both Hitchiti and Muskogee there are sounds that do not exist in English, and thus many Seminole words cannot be rendered accurately by our alphabet. Philologists get around this difficulty by using a special set of phonetic symbols. The present author has not used these symbols, which are unfamiliar to most people, but has attempted to transliterate the Seminole words as accurately as possible using English characters. Some words, in both Muskogee and Mikasuki, have tonal accents; certain syllables within these words must be pronounced with a higher pitch, or else with a high pitch falling to a low one. Thus, when either Seminole language is spoken there is a sing-song effect, much less pronounced than in some Oriental languages but nevertheless audible. No effort will be made to indicate tonal accents herein. Certain spellings, or rather mispellings, of Seminole words have become well-nigh standardized in Florida (e. g., coontie, chickee), and the author has not departed from previous usage; nor has he altered the spelling of Seminole names as commonly encountered in history books. It should be noted, however, that Indian names were badly mispronounced by the whites during the Seminole Wars. For example, one may read that a Mikasuki leader was named "Aripeka" or "Arpeika" or "Arpiucki"; but there is no sound of "r" in either of the Seminole languages, and the actual name was approximately Apayaka.

It may be seen that some Muskogee words are nearly or quite identical with their Mikasuki counterparts, while others are completely different therefrom.

A few words will illustrate the difference between the two Seminole languages:

English	Muskogee	Mikasuki
house ("chickee")	*chok-ko*	*chik-kee*
turban	*kadoboga*	*alabigee*
wagon	*toktsalitska*	*ahee-seneekee*
bread	*takla-eeki*	*palusti*
orange	*yalaha*	*yalahee*
onion	*tafumbi*	*tafumbi*
grits (corn gruel)	*osofkee*	*okthlee aspoksee*
bamboo	*koha*	*othlanee*
mud turtle	*tagokfumbee*	*yoktsabaloni*

A few Spanish words, usually much corrupted, crept into the Seminole languages, and especially into Mikasuki. These words are the names of things introduced by the Spaniards at an early date; and one may suppose that these names were borrowed by the ancestors of the Seminoles long before the exodus to Florida. Thus, the Mikasuki word for horse, *kawayi*, is from the Spanish *caballo*; the Muskogee word for cow, *waka*, and the Mikasuki, *waki*, are from the Spanish *vaca*; in both Muskogee and Mikasuki, the name for the tomato, *tomate*, is virtually identical with the Spanish. About a dozen other Seminole words are of Spanish origin. Just a few English words have been borrowed. The avocado, a tropical fruit, is called "alligator pear" by white Floridians and *haleegeta bia* by the Cow Creek Seminoles, while matches are called *matsi* in both Seminole languages. English names for days of the week, and also for the months, have likewise been borrowed, along with many place names.

The voice of the Seminole is always soft and low. When a group of these Indians gather about a fire for an evening chat, their conversation is almost whispered; and even one who understands the language must strain his ears to catch the words. Even the children talk quietly; and when they play, there is none of the squealing and yelling that white children seem to find so necessary. Seminoles do not yell at each other, nor do they use extravagant gestures when talking.

Although most Seminoles cannot read or write very well, many can speak English. Still others speak little English but nevertheless understand a good many words and phrases in that language. Most of the Seminoles, in fact,

111

know at least a little English, but many pretend total ignorance of the language, because they do not wish to talk to white strangers or to answer questions. Many of the Seminoles who speak good English are still difficult to understand, on account of their low, mumbling tones and their tendency to slur the sharper English sounds.

Some of the Seminoles can speak both Hitchiti and Muskogee, and a few can converse in both of these languages and in English as well.

The people whom we call "Seminoles" do not like that name, although they have become accustomed to it. Until recently they called themselves *Ikanyuksalgi*, a Muskogee term meaning "people of the peninsula." This name is still used by the Oklahoma Seminoles when referring to their Florida brethren. The Indians remaining in Florida now call themselves *Istichatee* in the Muskogee language, or *Yakitisee* in Mikasuki. Both names mean "red people."

SEMINOLE PERSONAL NAMES

Seminole personal names often sound strange and sometimes ludicrous to us. Actual Indian names were difficult for many white people to pronounce or write, and so most of the Seminoles found it necessary or at least desirable to have a name in the English language. Among many of the Seminoles, the father's surname is bestowed on all members of the immediate family, just as with us; this usage is not obligatory, however. Thus a recent Billy Bowlegs was the son of Billy Fewell, who was not a direct descendant of the original Bowlegs at all. Many Seminole surnames were adopted by the Indians several generations ago, while others were bestowed (often humorously) by white traders, hunters, and store-keepers.

Some Seminole names are in no way unusual. Thus we hear of Sam Huff, Billy Stuart, Joe Bowers, and Billy Smith. Other names are in English but are rather strange to our ears; for example, Barfield Johns, Frank Jim, Tony Tommie, and Willie Frank.

Many Seminole names combine an English first name with a surname translated from the Indian; for instance, Jim Gopher, Jack Tigertail, Charlie Snow, Bobby Chief,

A Seminole dugout canoe in use.

and Whitney Cypress.

As mentioned, the Seminoles are divided up into clans —groups of relatives tracing a common lineage to some remote ancestor. Most clans are named for some totem animal or manifestation of nature. Many members of the Tiger Clan have called themselves by the name of their totem animal; and so we hear of Tommy Tiger, Lucy Tiger, Ada Tiger, Cuffney Tiger, etc. Of course, the totem animal in this case was not really the tiger, which is Asiatic; it was the Florida panther, miscalled "tiger" by early white settlers.

Many Seminoles bear the names of tribal heroes, usually with an English first name. Examples are Richard Osceola, John Osceola, Willie Jumper, and Billy Bowlegs. While some of the present-day Osceolas believe they are descendants of the famous leader, others have simply adopted the name.

Some of the Seminole names are, or were, really titles of rank. Several Indians bear the name of Tustenuggee, which signified a sort of sub-chief. The meanings of most war titles, such as Emathla, Holahta, Fiksiko, and Hadjo, are no longer known to the Seminoles, who translate them literally if at all.

The white people often mispronounced or altered Seminole names, and the incorrect forms came to be used by the Indians themselves. Thus, "Osceola" was actually Asiyaholo, as explained previously.

A few other Seminole names, selected at random, are Josie Billie, Doctor Mill, Abraham Lincoln, Bird Fraser, Tiger Boy, Ingraham Billie, Cowboy Billie, Buffalo Tiger, Jackie Willie, Billy Willie, Willie Willie, William McKinley Osceola, Charle Dixie, Kissimmee Billie, Little Tiger-tail, Beets Tiger, Tiger Tiger, Willie Mexico Tiger, Keith Whoyah, Willie Jumper, Boy Jim, Doctor Johns, Rope Cypress, Conney Billie, Leepittee Billie, and Coffee Gopher. These names are useful in dealing with the whites; but each man has another name, a genuine Seminole name, bestowed upon him at the Green Corn Dance. An Indian generally called, say, Billie Tommie, may have a "real" name such as Tsala Tustenuggee or Yaha Chatee.

Wives of the more prominent Seminoles are usually called by their husbands' names. Thus we speak of Mrs. Albert Billie or Mrs. Charlie Cypress. Many Seminole women have only Indian names, however; examples are Chinasi, Sihoki, Ocelopi, and Suklatiki. Some other women's names, used in recent times, are Sally Cypress, Pocahontas Huff, Katie Smith, Courtney Parker, Missie Stick, Jim-sling, Rosa Billie, Gertrude Cypress, Laura Mae Jumper and Mrs. Miami Billie.

SEMINOLE PLACE NAMES IN FLORIDA

Seminole County, Florida, is named for the tribe, Osceola County for the famous leader, and Alachua County for one of the Seminole bands. Okeechobee County bears the Seminole name for the great lake of South Florida. Tallahassee, the state capital, was once a Seminole town, and the Indian name has persisted.

Okeechobee means "big water" in Mikasuki, while Tallahassee is "old town" in Muskogee. Here are a few Seminole place names and the original meanings; most of them are in Muskogee, somewhat mispronounced: Allapattah, alligator; Apopka, potato eating place; Bithlo, a dugout canoe; Chassahowitzka, hanging pumpkins; Chattahoochee, marked rocks; Chokolaskee, deserted house; Chuluota, fox den; Econfina, earth bridge(natural bridge; Efaw, dog; Fenholloway, high foot-log; Hatchineha, cypress tree; Illahaw, orange; Istachatta, red men; Loxahatchee, terrapin river; Narcoosee, a black bear; Okaloacoochee, little bad water; Ocklawaha, boggy; Panasoffkee, deep valley; Tsala Apopka, bass eating place; Wacahoota, cow barn; Wekiwachee, little spring (of water); Wekiwa, spring; Welaunee, yellow water; Wewahitchka, water view; Yalaha, orange.

Several Florida names end in -sassa. This Muskogee word means, literally, "some there." Wacasassa means "some cows there," or, we might say, "cow place." Thonotosassa means "flint place." Homosassa is generally translated "pepper place"; but the present-day Seminoles say that the original form of the name meant "whiskey place."

In some cases, the early white settlers just couldn't pronounce the Seminole names at all, and instead translated them. Thus, Wewahaiyayaki, "shining water," became Crystal River; Thlathlo-popka-hachi, "fish eating river," became Fish-eating Creek; Talak-chupco-hachi, "long beans river," became Peas Creek and finally Peace River; Yaha-hachi, "wolf river," became Wolf Creek.

The town of Aripeka, in Pasco County, is named for Apayaka, one of the last Seminole leaders. Emathla, in Marion County, probably was named for Tsala Emathla ("Charlie Emathla"), a Seminole who was killed by Osceola.

Micco, a town in Brevard County, means "chief." Micanopy, in Alachua County, originally meant "top chief"; it was the title of an important Seminole leader. Payne's Prairie, also in Alachua County, was named for King Payne, an early Seminole chief.

Not all Indian names in Florida are of Seminole origin, however. There were various Indian tribes in the state before the advent of the Seminoles. Not much is known of the earlier peoples, but some of their names have been handed down to the present day. Examples are Caloosa, Kissimmee, Miami, Myakka, Ocala, Ocilla, Pensacola, and Wakulla.

In several instances the Seminoles adopted place names that had been used by the earlier Indian tribes.

CHAPTER TWENTY-ONE

The Silver Springs Seminoles

The Silver Springs Seminoles are of considerable interest, for they demonstrate that the Indians can become successful and respected members of a community and yet retain their own ways which mean so much to them.

The Seminole colony at Silver Springs was started in 1935. Soon it was placed under the direction of Ross Allen. Several Indian families took up permanent residence at the springs. Various other Seminoles, mostly kinfolk of the residents, visit there for periods of time ranging from a few days to several weeks. Extra "chickees" have been built to accommodate them.

Several Seminoles have been born at Silver Springs; and the arrival of a little Indian is always a matter of moment, not only to the Seminoles but to the entire population of the community. One little lad was given a middle name of "Silver Springs"!

The encampment was provided with showers, a laundry room and sanitary conveniences. The Silver Springs Seminoles, some of whom are Baptists, then built a small church beside their settlement. Here a Seminole minister conducts services at intervals; and, in his absence, the Indians attend the First Baptist Church in Ocala, where they

117

are welcomed by the pastor and the entire congregation. Dressed in their brightest costumes, they always sit in the very front of the church and listen attentively to the sermon.

The men are not paid just for being at Silver Springs; instead they are provided with daily employment at good wages. Ross Allen's enterprises are constantly expanding, and there are always jobs for the Seminoles, especially in construction work. The women and children receive a small daily sum simply for their presence; and in addition, they keep all that they make from the sale of handicrafts.

The women are among the best of seamstresses. They make strikingly beautiful jackets and skirts from hundreds of strips of colored cloth, sewed together in an intricate pattern. These garments are in considerable demand and bring good sums. In addition, the women and children make dolls clothed in the traditional Seminole costume; and the men create models of dug-outs and Indian axes.

The handicrafts are derived from the Seminoles' own culture; these Indians are not set to making Alaskan totempoles, Sioux war-bonnets, Kiowa teepees, or Algonkin canoes.

For recreation the Silver Springs Seminoles often go to the movies in Ocala. The women are fond of visiting friends, while the men and boys like to hunt in the thick woods behind the encampment. Sometimes all the families wish to go down to the Everglades for a few days, generally at Christmas time or perhaps during the Green Corn Dance.

In short, the Silver Springs Seminoles lead a good, well-rounded life. They have a steady income, ideal working hours and conditions, plenty of wholesome recreation, medical attention when necessary, spiritual guidance, and freedom to live as they wish. They are clean, honest, and well-mannered. And most important, they maintain their dignity and self-respect; they are well adjusted to a way of life combining the best features of white and Indian culture.

CHAPTER TWENTY-TWO

Seminoles Outside Florida
Seminoles in the West

The reader may wonder what became of those Seminoles, several thousand in number, who submitted to removal from Florida, or who were captured and sent to the West during the period from about 1835 to 1858. They were taken to what was then a part of Arkansas, where, just as they had feared, they were set-down right among their traditional enemies, the Creeks. Now this territory seemed to be just about the most worthless expanse of land in the United States, and so the government rapidly dispossessed Indian tribes from all over the country and sent them there. Just west of the Seminoles were placed the Shawnee and Pottawatomie, to the southwest the Chickasaw, to the southeast the Choctaw, to the northwest the Kickapoo. Not far to the northeast, beyond the Creeks, were the Cherokees, and to the north, beyond another body of Creeks, were the Fox and the Osage. A little farther to the north and west were the Iowa, Pawnee, Otoe, Kaw, Tonkawa, Ponca, and others. As white settlements pushed westward the Comanche, Kiowa, Arapaho, and Cheyenne were uprooted from their native plains and sent to the same general region. The Modoc of California, the Nez

Percé of Oregon and Idaho, and the Chiricahua Apache from Arizona eventually met the same fate.

For a time life was very trying on the western reservation. The Seminoles had been put more or less under the jurisdiction of the Creek Indians, their enemies of long standing. Some of the Seminoles found this position intolerable, and so they moved away and settled as "squatters" on the nearby Cherokee reservation. Heading this rebellious faction were Coacoochee the Wildcat, who had led the tribe for a time after Osceola's capture; Alligator, who had engineered the Dade Massacre; and a Negro named John Cavallo. These three tried their best to remedy matters; in 1844 they went to Washington, D.C., to plead the Seminoles' cause, and Coacoochee wrote letters to the editors of newspapers, begging for help and a better deal. But their efforts were in vain; they got sympathy, but nothing more tangible. And so Coacoochee, Alligator and Cavallo secretly organized a group of Seminoles and Seminole Negroes. One night in 1850, the three, with several hundred followers, slipped off the reservation and headed southward. En route they picked up a band of Kickapoo Indians. After much rambling, they reached the vicinity of present-day Eagle Pass, Texas, where they crossed the Rio Grande River into Mexico. They were welcomed by the Mexican government, who gave them agricultural implements and a tract of land in the Santa Clara Mountains. They showed their gratitude by joining the Mexican army in a war against the Comanches and other Indians, and fought so well that they received formal thanks from the Mexican officers. The intrepid Seminoles defeated bands of Comanche and Apache Indians, revolutionists, smugglers, and slavers; and for the first time brought peace to the Mexican border country. After the Seminole wars came to an end, many of the refugees migrated back into the United States. The descendants of these Seminoles and Seminole Negroes still live along the Rio Grande River today, some in Mexico and some in Texas.

An historian, who has since been widely quoted, stated that the flight into Mexico was engineered and even led by the Negro, Abraham, who played such an important part in the Seminole Wars. This, however, was almost sure-

A Seminole family on Silver Springs river.

ly not the case, for Abraham is known to have repudiated Coacoochee's assumption of authority and to have advocated a peaceful settlement with the Creeks. Abraham died on the reservation in Oklahoma somewhere around 1870, about 20 years after the flight to Mexico took place.

The Seminoles who remained on the western reservation soon found themselves embroiled in the Civil War. The outbreak of this conflict, in 1861, had little effect on the Florida Seminoles, who were hidden away in the deep swamps. The Indians in the west were thrown into an uproar, however. Although most of the tribes there had no real reason to fight for either North or South, circumstances rendered it impossible for them to remain neutral. The Choctaws and Chickasaws promptly joined the Confederacy. The Cherokees were divided on the issue, but finally sided somewhat reluctantly with the South. One Cherokee leader rose to the rank of brigadier general in the Confederate army. Two-thirds of the Creeks joined the Confederacy, but the remainder, under the able chief, Opothle-yaholo, fought valiantly for the Union. Part of the Seminoles, under Halleck Tustenuggee, joined with Opothle-yaholo's Creeks and the Northern forces; while another part, led by John Jumper, fought for the South. Jumper eventually became a Confederate colonel.

After the Civil War, the western Seminoles became a self-governing body, generally called the "Seminole Nation". In 1906, mostly as a result of constant pressure from the United States government, all tribal organization came to an end, and the following year the "Indian Territory" was made into a state, Oklahoma.

Various treaties and laws had been passed, making it absolutely certain that the Indians and their descendants would remain on the reservation. And then Fate played on ironic trick—the "worthless" Oklahoma land proved to have some of the richest oil deposits in the country. Immediately there began a mad scramble to get the land back from the tribes, by any means. Reservations were pared down wherever possible, and the Indians were urged to sell their property for what must have been tempting sums. But many of the Indians were shrewd; they held to their lands and made a fortune. In 1942 an Oklahoma Sem-

The last resting place of a Seminole. Food and drink are placed beside the casket, and other possessions within.

inole named Peter Micco died, leaving an oil fortune of more than three million dollars. Another Oklahoma Seminole, Jackson Barnett, had died a few years previously, leaving an even larger sum.

SEMINOLES IN THE BAHAMAS AND CUBA

Even in the early 1800's, it must have been clear to many Florida Seminoles that their life was going to be mostly a series of struggles against the whites. The Negro allies of the Seminole, especially, were in an unpleasant situation, for, if captured, they faced a return to slavery or quite possibly execution. And so some of the Seminoles and Seminole Negroes determined to reach a country where they would not be molested. At that time the Seminoles knew how to build large ocean-going dug-outs, equipped with mast and sail, and capable of carrying 20 or 30 people. On several occasions between 1812 and 1840, groups of Seminoles and Seminole Negroes set out in these vessels and succeeded in reaching the Bahamas. Most of them landed at Red Bay, on the northwest coast of Andros Island. Some groups landed on the Joulter Cays but later moved to Red Bay. The refugees soon spread over northern Andros, which was wooded and virtually uninhabited. Perforce they reverted to a rather primitive existence, and hunted game with the bow and arrow.

On the other side of Andros lived many Bahaman Negroes, who soon came to fear the "wild men" from Florida and to tell outlandish tales about them. It was persistently rumored that the Seminoles were not only primitive, they were actually arboreal! The two groups remained aloof for quite a while, but eventually they inter-married. Today the Andros Islanders rarely show any Indian racial characters, but several Seminole customs, notably the manufacture of bows and arrows, have persisted.

The largest group of Seminoles to reach the Bahamas was headed by a "medicine man" named Scipio Bowlegs. In the year 1820, or thereabouts, he brought 150 or more Seminoles and Seminole Negroes to Andros. The descendants of Scipio Bowlegs and his followers have kept alive a very clear tradition of their origin and of the migration from Florida. A good many present-day Bahamans bear the surnames Bow-

enes on the Big Cypress Reservation. Note vast expanses of open marshland.

legs and Payne, which were common Seminole names at one time. An old Bahaman song still tells of "Bowlegs in the Trees".

It may be mentioned that the migration of Seminoles to the Bahamas, rather than to some other place, was not mere accident. In 1763, Spain lost Florida to the English and did not regain it until 1784. During the interim of British rule, relations between the Seminoles and the British were pleasant; and indeed these two peoples always were on friendly terms with each other. During the Second Seminole War, the Indians were certainly encouraged and quite possibly armed by the British. At that time there were many vessels plying the Caribbean, especially "wreckers" working out from bases in the British-controlled Bahamas. Seminoles could easily get transportation on these wreckers when large dug-outs were not at hand. The Indians knew quite well where the Bahamas lay, and were fairly certain that they would meet no hostile reception there.

Another group of Seminoles, hoping to avoid strife, set sail from Florida for Cuba, landing at Guanabacoa, a suburb of Havana. Their subsequent history remains unknown.

CHAPTER TWENTY-THREE

Concluding Remarks

It will be seen that the Florida Seminoles are not cultural-ly homogeneous. They differ among themselves in the extent to which they retain the old customs. They are divided into two linguistic groups and four political groups. The Big Cy-press people are more primitive than the others, slower to adopt innovations. Some of the Seminoles live on reserva-tions; a greater number do not. Some wear the native cos-tume exclusively, others frequently. Some are Christians, the majority are not. Some speak English well, many poorly, and others scarcely at all. A small number of Seminoles seem to be quite open with white strangers, but most are very re-served and may appear to be almost sullen.

The average person conceives an Indian to be a stern-faced, hook-nosed individual who wears a blanket and an eagle-feather bonnet, lives in a teepee, and who, when ad-dressed, replies "Ugh!" or "How!" This booklet and the pho-tographs therein should make it clear that the Seminole was and is very different from the popular concept. Actually, the numerous Indian tribes of the United States differed widely among themselves in appearance and customs. One thing many of the tribes have in common, however—a history of resistance to oppression, a tale of nearly hopeless struggle against overwhelming odds. Osceola and the Seminoles remind us in many ways of Geronimo and the Apaches; of Sitting Bull and the Sioux; of Chief Joseph and the Nez Percé; of Red Eagle and the Creeks; of Lone Wolf and the Kiowas. But only the Florida Seminole can say, "We are the unconquered; we never surrendered; we signed no peace treaty."

The Seminole Wars dragged to a close little more than 90 years ago. Among the Seminoles some bitterness yet remains, but it is vanishing. In 1938 the Florida Seminoles for the first time "recognized" the government of the United States. In this year a group of Seminole leaders, headed by Richard Osceola, expressed the willingness of their people to cooperate with the government. And when the United States entered World War II, the Florida Seminoles stated formally that their allegiance was to the Allies.

Today the Florida Seminoles have many friends. The Indian Agency, missionaries, various ministers, and many private citizens are always anxious to aid the Seminoles. There is a society called the Seminole Indian Association of Florida, composed of business men and other citizens who for years have contributed toward the welfare of the Indians. Seminole children are welcomed in white schools. The Miami Herald has always taken an interest in the Seminoles, and in 1949 it published articles citing the wants and needs of the Indians. The response was overwhelming; food, clothing, blankets, much - needed water pumps, children's toys, and many other donations poured in and were distributed. An association of airplane pilots gave many presents to the Seminoles, who had often aided fliers forced down in the Everglades or Big Cypress Swamp. Many other instances could be cited to show that the general public is not entirely oblivious to the tragic history and unfortunate plight of the Florida Seminoles. Certainly the picture could be much darker.

At the present time, in 1956, it seems that the Seminoles are on the way to becoming citizens in fact as well as in name. We can at least hope that these original Americans, social outcasts for so long, will again become Americans.